Sex and Romance

A Lifetime of Learning, Book 3

Mark Andre Alexander

Make clear distinctions,
and examine all things well.
*The Golden Verses of
Pythagoras*

THE SCHOOL OF
PYTHAGORAS™
Auburn, CA

Published by Mark Andre Alexander
P.O. Box 5286, Auburn, CA 95604-5286

First Edition

Library of Congress Cataloging-in-Publication Data

Alexander, Mark Andre, 1956-
Sex and romance: a lifetime of learning, book 3 / by Mark Andre Alexander

p. cm. — (A Lifetime of Learning, Book 3)
ISBN 978-1-937597-22-1

An Amazon.Com Kindle eBook

Cover design by Melinda De Ross: www.coveredbymelinda.com

Some photos and illustrations licensed from Thinkstock.com.

Version 2_3

Formatted for iPad and other tablets.

Thanks to my readers: Bree, Scott, Frank, and Christine. Also, thanks to BubbleCow.Com for their great book editing services at a reasonable price.

Go to MarkAndreAlexander.Com to get FREE podcasts and other benefits.

Subscribe to the *Creating Your Life* YouTube channel.

SEX AND ROMANCE

A Lifetime of Learning, Book 3

Make clear distinctions,
and examine all things well.

*The Golden Verses of
Pythagoras*

For Bree and HK,
and those who Quest

CONTENTS

About This Series

How many times have we said it to ourselves?

If I only knew then what I know now?

This series of little books, titled *A Lifetime of Learning*, gives my personal, and admittedly idiosyncratic, discoveries over the years. They are packed full of the gems I'd wished I'd known in my teens.

In many cases, knowing then what I know now would have saved me time, money, and heartache; would have enriched me, and given me greater personal freedom.

This third book, on *Sex and Romance*, distills what I have learned about some of the great questions:

— What are the differences between men and women?

— What mistakes can we easily fall into when we confuse sex and romance?

— And what is the truth about love, friendship, and happiness?

The publishing imprint I have chosen, The School of Pythagoras, points to the quest for the fundamental nature of Truth.

This series is dedicated to those of you on that quest.

Introduction

We mistake sex for romance.
Guys are taught that pushing a girl
up against a wall is romance.
Sex is easy; you can do it
with anyone, yourself, with batteries.
John C. Moffi

If you learn two things from this little book, then let it be these:

**1) When it comes to sex, men and women
exercise judgment differently.**

**2) People who seek romance are
actually aiming for joy and happiness.**

Few experiences in life can send us soaring into the sky or crashing into the ground like sex and romance.

Young people are impressionable. They take cues from adults about expected behavior. So it should not be surprising that many boys and girls are sexually active at an early age.

But rarely do adults give essential truths about sex and romance.

We do often give boys and girls clinical truths, about pregnancy and sexually transmitted diseases (STDs). But is that all they need?

Boys stumble around trying to impress girls. Girls awkwardly expect boys to understand them. And a boy who likes other boys, or girls who like other girls, can find sex and romance even more confusing.

Whatever your unique orientation, you should be able to apply some, if not most, of the insights you find here.

You will find this little book has new ways of looking at old truths.

How This Little Book Can Help

We live in a world that often doesn't want to admit that men and women are different. But differences are valuable. And understanding those differences in a positive light helps people understand each other.

This little book describes those differences.

It will help you know when you are being used.

It should help prevent you from using others.

And it will help build your confidence when experiencing romance with others.

However, this book is not a sex manual. You will find no recommendations about sexual activity and its relationship to romance. Plenty of manuals already exist, if that is your interest.

Here is a glimpse into what follows:

Chapter 1: Sex... tells a simple little sex story.

Chapter 2: ...and Intoxication discloses something intimate about you.

Chapter 3: What Girls Should Know About Boys reveals secrets that girls should not have to learn the hard way.

Chapter 4: What Boys Should Know About Girls reveals secrets that boys should not have to learn the hard way.

Chapter 5: Male Consciousness clues you in to the male side of you.

Chapter 6: Female Consciousness clues you in to the female side of you.

Chapter 7: Gay, Lesbian, Transgender, and the Rest provides pithy advice.

Chapter 8: Romance, Part 1 shows how dating can be so much more.

Chapter 9: Love talks about the many different kinds of love, ending with a focus on unconditional love.

Chapter 10: Marriage presents, among other things, the four questions you should ask yourself before deciding to marry.

Chapter 11: Romance, Part 2 outlines how romance should not end with marriage.

Chapter 12: Happiness draws important distinctions among pleasure, contentment, true happiness, practicing virtues, and the supreme value of friendship.

Now for a simple little sex story…

Chapter 1

Sex...

*I have no objection to anyone's sex life as long as
they don't practice it in the street and frighten the horses.*
Oscar Wilde

In my early 20s I was in a couple of rock bands.

I had a Fender Rhodes piano with 88 keys. Pity the
poor keyboard players who have to be their own
roadies and carry their own bulky instruments.

The first band was so dysfunctional we didn't have a name and played only one party. But it only took one party to discover that, no matter how dysfunctional your band, you still get groupies.

> We were in the middle of a song when she came up to me, thin and dark-haired, holding a beer, and whispered in my ear, "I want you."

> That's all it took.

> The next break, we walked down the street where we found a house under construction and we cavorted (it's a real word, look it up) in several ways.

> Later, I drove her home, but she wasn't finished, so we had to pull over on the side of the road to continue our cavorting ways.

> I was a young man, and not very thoughtful. She was a young woman, and yet she wasn't very thoughtful either. We both simply indulged our animal urges, without much reflection.

> I did not see her again until a few years later when she walked up, said hello, reminded me who she was, and said she had given up drinking alcohol because it affected her ability to discriminate.

> I felt slightly embarrassed, but didn't think too much about it.

*Some years later, I learned that
another profession also brings out groupies...
teaching.*

When I was set to teach my first English Composition course in a university as a graduate teaching assistant, a fellow T. A., a female, told me something I had never considered. She explained that as a somewhat decent looking male, I should know that half the women in any class I taught would be in love with me.

I found that hard to believe, but in time, I found it partially true. Maybe not love, but at least lust. Apparently, that's just the way it is.

I became popular as a teacher because I went out of my way to make English interesting. You can imagine how half the students entering an English class involving grammar and spelling would arrive already hating the class.

So I spent that first class completely shattering the mold of every English class and English teacher they'd ever hated. I was passionate, made them laugh, and demonstrated how everything I would teach them would have practical value.

I would show them the value of language in a way that would not waste their time. I demonstrated how important their language skills were, and how they would be judged in the business world by how they used or misused language.

I promised to show them how important getting the right preposition was. If they didn't, they risked saying something not only wrong, but also embarrassing.

For example, I would write two sentences on the chalkboard and say to them as I wrote:

You might think that

*They laughed at him when he came **into** the room*

was the same as

*They laughed at him when he came **in** the room.*

But one preposition expresses movement and the other signifies location.

That's quite a difference.

And if you don't know the difference, you may have co-workers laughing at you behind your back.

The students loved this kind of thing.

> I left my graduate studies to teach at a business college. It was where people come after they find out they need more business skills, but who don't want to go to college. Also included were middle-aged people on rehabilitation insurance programs needing to get retrained.

> So I had female students from 18 to 55.

> And it wasn't long before some of them began hitting on me in that subtle, smiley, look-at-me-in-this-tight-dress way.

But I couldn't see having an affair with a current student in my class. And I couldn't trust that such a relationship would remain discreet. Females have a way of demonstrating that they own a man when they are secretly shagging him.

As long as they were my students, in my classroom, they were off limits.

I taught a 20-week English class, a ten-week Business Writing class, and a couple of others. In my first 20-week class, there was a 22-year-old woman who began making sure I noticed her.

Sometimes she would make slightly suggestive comments, but nothing very overt.

The class began in June and ended in October. Although I had thoughts about her now and then, it was only in the last couple of weeks that I began thinking seriously about her implied offer. She was curvy and voluptuous. She knew how to exude sexuality. And a guy without a girlfriend can only resist for so long.

The college held an annual Halloween party with prizes for the best costume. My female roommate at that time loaned me a dress, a bra, and some nylons, got out her makeup, and worked around the beard I wore. I put one of her scarves on my head. You should have seen me with lipstick and eye makeup, cuddly cute in scarf and beard.

The women at the college went kind of wild when they saw me walk into the outside courtyard where the party was.

They kept trying to see if I was wearing any underwear with those nylons (I wasn't). I felt like Marilyn Monroe holding my dress down against this insistent street fan of women.

One woman in her fifties even pinched my butt.

My former sexy student (the class had ended a week earlier) was talking with another female and looking my way, leering a bit, and when I walked up, they shut up and smiled.

From the little I overheard, it was obvious they were gossiping about what she might do to me under that dress.

I won first prize, not surprisingly.

After the party, it was time to go upstairs to the classrooms. It was the end of the day. An enclosed stairway led from the courtyard up to a door on the second floor.

This young woman followed me up the stairs and, noticing that no one else could hear us, she decided to make a move.

"You know what I'd like?" she said.

"What's that?" I asked.

"I'd like to [expletives deleted]."

I caught my breath, stopped, turned, and she half-smiled, shooting me a lust-filled look. She leaned forward and brushed her lips against mine.

She then flicked her tongue lightly across them while no one was looking. She leaned forward for a more serious kiss, brushing herself against me before pulling away.

I don't quite remember what was said after that, other than we set the time two days later at my home (she lived quite a distance away and I lived within walking distance from the college).

Before leaving she asked me, if she brought me a gift the next day, would I promise to wear it at school the day after? It was the day we'd set to have our confidential liaison.

I said sure.

The next day she brought me a pair of her black lace panties.

The day after that I came to school wearing them. I discovered ladies' panties don't quite fit the way men's underwear fit.

And I haven't worn women's underwear since.

But it excited her.

I wonder sometimes that some women like to put a mark on a man, a sort of ownership, even a secret ownership.

The next day, she arrived at my front door and I let her in. We didn't say much as I led her to my bedroom. We kicked off our shoes. She turned up her head and we kissed again, but with more heat. She pulled me close and I felt her body, from breasts to thighs, push against mine.

And my body responded, my heart starting to race, my breath catching.

My hands became tangled in her wavy hair as I clutched the back of her head. Her tongue played inside my lips, over my teeth. Her breath in my mouth, and the smell of her, like gardenias, but more musky.

Her taste like ripe fallen pears.

There was no hesitation, no doubt, no reticence.

She pulled back slightly from the kiss, my hand now on her neck, turning my head, pulling her in to nuzzle my ear. Her kisses down my neck, her hand undoing my shirt.

I pushed her back, she removed my shirt. I removed her blouse, then her bra.

Revealed magnificence. My breath caught, then deepened.

She, kissing the middle of my chest, and I, cupping her and rubbing my thumb over her gently. My fingers on her sternum, feeling her heart pulse. Her skin delicate and slightly moist.

She, undoing my belt while lightly kissing and licking my solar plexus. Her nails sharp against my lower back. I, playing with her hair.

She, arching her back, looking up at me, smiling, one hand stroking the back of my thigh.

I, looking down at her, half-closing my eyes and...

...and...

...and how do you feel right now?

Is your heart pumping loudly in your ears?

Is your breath faster and shallower?

Do you have some kind of intoxicating substance coursing through your veins, heating your blood?

Chapter 2

...and Intoxication

*It is impossible to live pleasurably
without living wisely, well, and justly,
and it is impossible to live wisely, well, and justly
without living pleasurably.*
Epicurus

Isn't it amazing how little black squiggles on white can produce an effect in you similar to alcohol intoxication?

Think about it.

Don't you feel like you've ingested a shot of liquor or some other kind of drug?

Something that warms your blood, stimulates your heart, and distracts your attention?

> What amazes me is how rare it is that we warn our children about the dangerously intoxicating effects of sex.
>
> Schools teach the clinical aspects, but rarely do you hear of anyone talking about the drug-induced aspects of sex.

> > *How you can lose your discrimination when sexually aroused.*
> >
> > *And how, like alcohol, it can bring out strong emotional reactions like sexual jealousy.*

> And how when sexual arousal is mixed with alcohol or drugs it can be even more powerful.
>
> Discrimination can fly out the window.
>
> And the next day, the denials begin.
>
> I wonder whether when a child is around age twelve, every responsible parent should have a talk with his or her child about the intoxicating effects of sex.
>
> And the possibly dangerous consequences of indulging in sex before having experience and maturity in relationships.

How many young people have ended up with children not realizing the consequences of sexual intoxication?

How many young men have refused to take responsibility for those children, because, you know, it was just sex, and it's not his fault she wasn't taking birth control?

How many young women had their hearts romantically open, and somehow thought sex would lead to greater romance?

And instead they find themselves with a child?

How many young men find themselves embarrassed after sex, and can think of nothing more than quickly getting away?

How many young women take the young man's embarrassment as a sign that something is deeply wrong with themselves?

All because they failed to recognize some essential truths:

> — Sexual energy is intoxicating. Literally, chemically intoxicating.

> — It affects judgment in the same way that alcohol affects judgment.

> — Boys and girls are different, emotionally as well as physically and mentally.

Understanding these differences can help parents and youths (and some of us aging adults) get a better handle on avoiding some major stumbling blocks in life.

The next two chapters provide some tips on what parents may consider discussing with their children. And these chapters may also help us all reflect on how, in our youth, we did some silly and thoughtless things.

Chapter 3

What Girls Should Know About Boys

I think men talk to women so they can sleep with them and women sleep with men so they can talk to them.
Jay McInerney

Girls and boys are different, no matter how much we want to believe otherwise.

Clearly, they should both have the same opportunities in life to pursue the lives and careers they want. A healthy society works to protect and support anyone's desire to pursue any healthy path.

But a healthy society also acknowledges the differences between boys and girls. If it does not, it risks misunderstandings that can affect the rise of healthy relationships.

Every girl should know some of the key differences between how girls relate to sex and romance, and how boys relate. The differences can be startling.

In this chapter, we speak of girls of all ages.

1. Sexual excitement is intoxicating like alcohol or drugs.

> It will cloud your judgment, inhibit critical thinking, and make you do things later that you may regret.

> And the consequences for girls are usually more devastating than for boys.

2. Sex carries profound emotional feelings with it, but many boys DO NOT feel this in the way girls do.

> Boys tend to be more detached from emotions than girls. Boys usually attach no meaning to sex other than the physical pleasure of it.

> In fact, it is often worse than that. Some boys who have discovered sex can turn into disgustoids in human form.

Many boys will fantasize having sex with almost every female they see.

This means that boys begin looking at girls as OBJECTS for their own sexual pleasure. They will often consciously and unconsciously dehumanize girls, simply because they are too young to be all that thoughtful of a girl's feelings.

3. *Sex is usually a physical thing for boys.*

Sex is pleasure for boys, rarely involving emotions. And once boys climax, which is often very quick, the intoxication rapidly ends.

Boys will often feel embarrassed being intimate and find some way to leave.

They often do not know how to behave after sex. Being embarrassed, they simply want to get away and forget about everything.

Boys can subconsciously seek out girls for caring and nurturing. And they will mix sex with that drive. But since they don't know what drives them, such intimacy is simply confusing.

Boys are just as confused about intimacy as girls. And the simplest way for them to deal with that confusion is to get away.

4. *Many boys have little problem having sex with a girl and then forgetting about her and her feelings.*

Since boys are very likely to see girls as sexual objects for their gratification, they are generally clueless and careless about a girl's pleasure and feelings.

Intimate feelings are uncharted territories for boys. They don't have experience with how to deal with such feelings.

So they walk away.

5. *When a girl wants to indulge in sex with a boy, she will have to be direct and explicit with him about anything she wants beyond sex.*

> Boys rarely perceive indirect communications. They do not understand a girl's feelings. They rarely have a sense of a romantic future.

> And even if a girl tells a boy what she wants, a boy may not understand.

> Or just as likely, under the intoxicating effects of sex, he will just say what he thinks the girl wants to hear.

> So he can get what he wants to get.

> Remember, sex is intoxicating. It affects the judgment and discrimination. Boys will say what they don't mean while intoxicated.

6. *Boys and girls usually don't get a true and clear sense of themselves until they are in their mid-20s.*

> Until then, girls are more likely to misjudge the intentions of boys and what they really need or want from them.

And if they indulge in sexual intoxication, and a girl lets a boy video her sexual activity, she should not be surprised if it ends up on the Internet.

7. Most boys do not have the maturity to handle a girl getting pregnant.

And girls don't want to be single parents.

Girls should wait until they are able to handle sexual intoxication before getting into compromising sexual situations.

Girls may want to review the four questions in the chapter, "Marriage," before they choose to have sex with a certain boy.

8. Boys, even good ones whose judgment is clouded, may take advantage of a girl if she gets intoxicated and passes out at a party.

This truth is sad, I know, but too many women can tell a girl how it happened to them.

Intoxication shuts down the morals and judgment.

Many boys can get caught up in animalistic group urges and exploit girls at parties. And who knows; they may decide to video what they do while the girl is drunk and passed out, then post it on the Internet.

9. A boy will rarely care about a girl just because she gives him sex.

In fact, he is more likely to stop thinking about the girl once she's given in.

Sex is not an effective way to make a boy like a girl.

Remember—sex for boys is an act of personal pleasure. Not a romantic encounter.

Their feelings are limited to their physical pleasure. Which explains why they often seem to care little about how much physical pleasure a girl is receiving.

10. *There are plenty of boys, especially handsome and nice ones, who have bets about taking a girl's virginity.*

Some are even trying to be the first to have sex with a hundred or even a thousand girls.

They will lie to have sex with a girl.

A girl is just a number to them.

11. *If a girl engages in sex, she should ask that it be for her pleasure as well as his.*

Girls will probably have to be direct about what they want, about what pleases them. Boys often don't have a clue.

Boys often need training. And a sense of caring. Often, that sense of caring does not develop for many years, without help.

12. *Older men can be more fun and considerate, but they can still be boys inside.*

Read the chapter "Rites of Passage" in *Creating Your Life: A Lifetime of Learning* to get details on why this happens.

Older men can easily lie when they say they will someday leave their wife or family for a girl. "Someday" never comes if he is getting what he wants from a girl.

Actions speak. Mere words do not always lead to actions.

13. *Girls will learn quickly that they can manipulate boys with sexual intoxication.*

Yes, girls can stimulate a boy, and learn ways of controlling or influencing his behavior.

But a girl should be careful.

She will sooner or later run into one who will be insecure enough to get violent.

14. *If a boy seriously hits a girl, she should not expect him to love.*

She should get help immediately, and prepare to leave after the first time he hits.

Especially if they have a child.

Hitting may be just the start.

In many cases, it happens over and over again.

* * *

Here is one more thing to consider: *Overindulgence in sex can potentially have bad physical and psychological effects.*

> Just as overindulgence in alcohol or any drug can be harmful, so can overindulgence in intoxicating sex.

> Too much sex for the sake of sex can degrade you physically, emotionally, and mentally. It can affect your personal character, as well as your reputation.

> But less obviously, sexual intoxication, and the lack of judgment that goes with it, can result in physical diseases.

> Furthermore, sex is often demeaning when not accompanied by love and romance.

> Take, for instance, any kind of pornography. The Internet is full of it.

> Have you noticed the trend of how everyone who participates in pornography indulges in snarling, animalistic behavior?

> Is this really an elevating experience?

> Or is it all about exploiting base behaviors?

> How do you feel after you indulge in pornography?

> Do you feel a growing crassness in your consciousness?

Do you merely accept how 90% of what you are seeing is actually exploiting people, often young people, in a predatory way?

Do you like what you and your friends become when you overindulge in pornography?

Remember the insight from *Creating Your Life: A Lifetime of Learning*:

> *You move toward and become like what you put your attention on.*

Do you really want to become like those gyrating bodies in porn videos?

"Consuming pornography does not lead to more sex, it leads to more porn. Much like eating McDonalds every day will accustom you to food that (although enjoyable) is essentially not food, pornography conditions the consumer to being satisfied with an impression of extreme sex rather than the real."
Virginia Despentes

* * *

Girls tend to develop their inner selves more easily and more quickly. Boys tend to focus on their external selves and pleasures.

For this reason, girls tend to concern themselves more with inner feelings and the meaning of relationships. On the other hand, boys tend to concern themselves with external activities and their relationships with exterior objects.

Even the most well-intentioned boys can easily objectify girls.

Now we will review what boys should know about girls.

After that, we'll delve deeper into the differences between male consciousness and female consciousness.

Chapter 4

What Boys Should Know About Girls

Men always want to be a woman's first love,
women like to be a man's last romance.
Oscar Wilde

**Boys and girls are different, no matter how much we
want to believe otherwise.**

We've just reviewed what girls should know about boys. But boys should understand a few things about girls as well. Boys are often unaware of the forces they can unwittingly set into motion.

In this chapter, we speak of boys of all ages.

1. Sexual excitement is intoxicating like alcohol or drugs.

> It will cloud a boy's judgment, inhibit critical thinking, and make him do things that later he may regret.

> And the consequences boys bring down on girls are usually more devastating in ways they can hardly comprehend. That includes triggering unexpected emotions and attachments, as well as risking a pregnancy.

2. While sex is a physical thing for a boy, it can be a strong emotional thing for a girl.

> Girls can easily develop strong emotional attachments.

> Think about it: Sex is an external thing for boys. But it is an internal thing for a girl.

> Boys feel it outside. Girls feel it inside.

> You can get a better insight into this fact by reading the chapter on "Female Consciousness."

> But for now, realize that girls are not as detached as boys. Sex does not just end for girls when it ends for boys.

Where it's like jumping on and off a bus for boys, it's more like a long road trip for girls. Boys may get off the bus, but girls are still riding it and wondering where the boy has gone.

3. Girls will almost ALWAYS attach more meaning to sex than boys will.

Schools will talk about sexually transmitted diseases (STDs) and pregnancy as dangers (and they are, no matter what kind of birth control used).

But boys need to know that girls can form strong attachments when having sex with boys.

They will almost always expect more from boys than they realize.

Girls experience a more profound intimacy during sex.

4. Boys will, more often than not, cause emotional damage to girls when they have sex.

Boys think they are just having sex.

But because a girl has let a boy inside of her, she can experience sex as having a more intimate meaning.

Boys don't realize how detached they are from their own feelings. How easy it is to let go and move on.

And because boys do not always connect to their feelings as do girls, boys think girls feel the same way they do.

Girls do not feel the same way that boys do. They feel transparently and more deeply.

A girl's feelings are more likely to be connected to subtle changes in a boy's words, actions, and behaviors.

5. *Girls may not tell boys directly how deeply and emotionally they feel.*

Girls will amplify any small endearment boys give them to mean something much more than intended.

Any little gift becomes a world of meaning. Girls will imagine more than what a boy actually means.

Girls will interpret a boy's external actions as internal feelings.

Girls believe in subtext. Not what a boy says, but what he implies with what he says and does not say. Girls can attach meanings to things in ways boys have no clue about.

6. *Boys will learn quickly that girls can manipulate them with sexual intoxication.*

Some girls will purposely get boys jealous so that they will fight other boys over them. Some insecure girls find this twisted game entertaining. The game is called, "How much does my boyfriend love me?"

The object of this game is to make boys crazy, not with love or lust, but with jealousy.

"Does he love me enough to fight for my love and honor?"

Boys get played easily and end up fighting some unsuspecting guy. Meanwhile, the girl leans back, takes in the drama, and feels loved.

* * *

Here are a couple of other thing boys should know:

If a boy sees an overly intoxicated girl at a party or one who has passed out, if he has sex with her, he is committing rape.

No matter what he believes.

No matter what she has said.

No matter what his friends say or do.

Sex with an unconscious girl is rape.

If a boy and his buddies see girls as simple objects for their sexual pleasure and abuse, then he and his buddies are behaving in an uncivilized manner.

Especially if they hit girls; this is a sign that they are not men, but immature boys.

* * *

As you can see, boys and girls can approach sex and romance in starkly different ways: Boys more physically and mentally, girls more emotionally.

(That's not to say there aren't girls who can be just as physical as boys.)

It's no wonder that John Gray entitled his bestselling (but often awkward and somewhat out-of-date) book, *Men are from Mars, Women are from Venus.*

But both boys and girls can grow properly with parental guidance and understanding, whether by a parent, a teacher, a friend, or a thoughtful lover.

Given the differences between boys and girls, it's worth going deeper into the differences between male consciousness and female consciousness.

It's especially important to keep in mind that...

Everyone,
both male and female,
possess and can express
both kinds of consciousness,
male and female.

Chapter 5

Male Consciousness

*I just feel like every kid is growing up too fast
and they're seeing too much.
Everything is about sex, and that's fine for me.
I'm not saying I don't like it.
But I don't think it should be everywhere,
where kids are exposed to everything sexual.
Because they have to have some innocence;
there's just no innocence left.*
Ellen DeGeneres

**Male consciousness tends to be externally oriented, linear
and focused on a goal, direct and explicit in expression.**

Life is full of variety, more than we know or recognize. Male consciousness tends to manifest in male bodies, and female consciousness tends to manifest in female bodies.

But both can exist in each. Often, one predominates. But the potential is there.

If you think about it, you have seen female consciousness expressed in a male body, and male consciousness expressed in a female body. Furthermore, sometimes even strong males display a female side to their consciousness, just as occasionally females display a strong male side to their consciousness.

In this chapter we focus on the characteristics of male consciousness.

*Symbolically,
male consciousness tends to be a line,
while female consciousness tends to be a circle.*

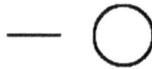

— ◯

It seems nature exhibits these symbols in male and female anatomy.

Both male consciousness and female consciousness have positive virtues while being quite different.

Here's a humorous video about one characteristic of the male consciousness. The video is called *IBM - Keep It Simple*:

https://tinyurl.com/sarvid1

Male Consciousness: External, Linear, Focused, Direct, and Explicit

Male consciousness tends to focus on the external world.

Men gravitate toward:

— external activities,

— sports and politics,

— tools and electronics,

— cars and machines,

— mechanisms and wireless controls,

— building things and taking them apart,

— model ships and airplanes,

— remote-control cars, airplanes, and helicopters,

— playing soldier, shooting guns, fishing, hunting, running around, and being rowdy.

Many men find joy in putting together complex electronic equipment, and then mastering the complexity of a sophisticated remote control.

They can love the competitiveness of sports, memorizing baseball statistics, reciting a litany of background data on players and teams, their history, and wins and losses.

Males are goal-oriented problem solvers. This is an evolutionary advantage that is useful when they need to hunt for food or protect their family or community.

They like to solve problems and fix things.

They love to achieve goals and win.

When men speak as boys, they may tend to be too direct and unsophisticated. They need to be "civilized" into being more aware and sensitive to the effects their words have on others.

Male consciousness tends to be relatively simple, playful, and action-oriented. Self-reflection, consideration of feelings, and examination of inner motivations are rarely the male default setting. Often those behaviors need more attention.

Once a high school graduating class was taken on a camping trip in the desert.

A creative writing teacher decided to lead the students on an exercise to develop their imaginations, to make them more sensitive.

They were given notebooks, pens, candles, and matches. The instructions were simple: Walk a short way into the desert, find a place alone, and proceed to "discover yourself."

What did the girls do?

They followed instructions.

What did the boys do?

Since the assignment baffled them, they gathered together, piled up their notebooks, lit them with the matches...

...and started a bonfire.

In *Dave Barry's Complete Guide to Guys,* the author tells a story that illustrates, in a funny way, one key difference between male consciousness and female consciousness.

A young man and a young woman have been dating each other for many months.

One evening while he drove her home, she says, "You know, as of tonight, we've been together for six months."

Silence.

She begins thinking that what she says bothers him, that perhaps he thinks she's placing some kind of obligation on him, pushing him into something.

And he's thinking, *Wow. Six months.*

And she goes off examining their relationship and her motives, where they are going...

Marriage? Children?

And he's thinking, *Six months. That means we met after I took the car in for service, and...wow, look at the odometer. I'm way overdue for an oil change...*

And she's thinking about what he might want from the relationship, issues of intimacy and commitment and...

He's thinking about how he may have been ripped off by a car mechanic...

And she's thinking, *He looks mad...Perhaps I said something too soon...*

When the two of them start actually talking again, is it any surprise that the young man essentially says, "Huh?" while she's trying to explain that she didn't mean anything by what she said.

My synopsis cannot do justice to the original story. Dave Barry's book is very funny precisely because, as outrageous as it sometimes is, he bases his humor on some very true and fundamental differences between male consciousness and female consciousness.

Male consciousness tends to be, and expects others to be, explicit. Male consciousness is not naturally responsive to subtext.

We will save examples of this distinction for the next chapter on "Female Consciousness."

A Note about the War Against Boys

In the United States, a disturbing trend is happening in the public schools. Competition and risk are frowned upon, while the value of feelings are elevated. Games like dodge ball and active recess activities are being eliminated.

Natural boy-based behaviors are labeled "aggressive" and anything aggressive is deemed bad by definition.

Culturally, there appears to be a concerted effort to stigmatize all playful use of guns. Zero-tolerance policies punish boys for pretending to have guns.

Even drawing the picture of a gun or forming one with your hand can result in suspension or expulsion.

Here are more stories from 2013:

> A 10-year-old boy in Pennsylvania was suspended for using an imaginary bow and arrow.

> An 8-year-old Arizona boy was threatened with expulsion because of his **drawings** of ninjas and Star Wars characters, and his interest in zombies.

> A 7-year-old boy in Maryland was **suspended** for chomping a Pop Tart into the shape of a gun.

> A 6-year-old boy in Colorado was charged with "**sexual harassment**" for kissing a girl.

(Search the Internet for such stories. They are legion.)

Increasingly, boys are seen as defective girls.

When male consciousness is denigrated in full, the results can be catastrophic. That male energy *will* come out, in unexpected and inappropriate ways.

Think back to the first book in this series, *Creating Your Life: A Lifetime of Learning.* Remember the section on how boys and girls go through a rite of passage into becoming men and women?

Here's an excerpt from that section:

> Has it ever occurred to you that the reason that there are so many boys in men's bodies is because these boys **never** went through a rite of passage TO CHANGE THEIR PICTURE?
>
> GIRLS HAVE A NATURAL BIOLOGICAL EVENT THAT USHERS THEM INTO WOMANHOOD.
>
> WHAT DO BOYS HAVE?
>
> THEY USED TO HAVE FATHERS WHO TOOK THEM HUNTING OR CAMPING, OR DID SOMETHING THAT RITUALLY USHERED THEM INTO BEING A MAN. AN ADULT MALE WITH ADULT MALE RESPONSIBILITIES.
>
> HOW OFTEN THESE DAYS IS THAT PARTICULAR RITE OF PASSAGE MISSED?

In the U.S., we live in an age that attacks traditional male practices that initiate boys into men.

What are the consequences?

Boys in men's bodies. Boys who do not know how to appropriately channel male energy. Boys who are expected to behave in the civil ways that come much more naturally to the female consciousness.

In short, males become confused about their roles in society.

If you question these statements, ask any woman not immersed in academic studies.

For more information on this topic, I recommend a book by a feminist scholar, Christina Hoff Summers, called *The War Against Boys: How Misguided Policies are Harming Our Young Men.*

Also, you can check out an indepth C-Span interview with her:

https://tinyurl.com/sarvid2

Now that we have more insight into male consciousness, let's turn to female consciousness.

Chapter 6

Female Consciousness

*I often think that a slightly exposed shoulder
emerging from a long satin nightgown
packs more sex than two naked bodies in bed.*
Bette Davis

Female consciousness tends to be internally oriented,
circular and diffuse, indirect and implicit in expression,
with an emphasis on subtext.

Life is full of variety, more than we know or recognize. Female consciousness tends to manifest in female bodies, and male consciousness tends to manifest in male bodies.

But both can exist in each. Often one predominates. But the potential is there.

If you think about it, you have seen male consciousness expressed in a female body, and female consciousness expressed in a male body. Furthermore, sometimes even strong females display a male side to their consciousness, just as occasionally males display a strong female side to their consciousness.

In this chapter, we focus on the characteristics of female consciousness.

> *Symbolically,*
> *male consciousness tends to be a line,*
> *while female consciousness tends to be a circle.*

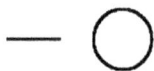

— ◯

It seems nature exhibits these symbols in male and female anatomy.

Both male consciousness and female consciousness have positive virtues while being quite different.

Here's a humorous video called *It's Not About the Nail* about one characteristic of the female consciousness:

https://tinyurl.com/sarvid3

Female Consciousness: Internal, Circular, Indirect, Diffuse, and Implicit (Subtext)

Female consciousness tends to focus on the internal world.

Women gravitate toward:

— internal activities,

— expressions of feelings,

— explorations of relationships,

— communicating indirectly,

— sensitivity to nonverbal cues,

— environmental and personal aesthetics,

— cultivating the tasteful and beautiful,

— awareness of the whole, the Big Picture.

Women can communicate with each other in ways that men have no clue what is going on. Men, if you want a much-needed education in female consciousness, ask any woman in your life the following question:

*Do women nonverbally communicate
with each other in ways that
men are absolutely clueless about?*

The answer is a universal yes.

Take the time to ask for details and examples. The conversation should be a revelation to you.

Women are much more naturally adapted to the awareness and expression of *subtext*. Every man should take the time to understand how subtext works.

*Men are affected by subtext all the time
and don't know it.*

Subtext can manifest in several ways:

— Indirect meanings underlying the spoken or written word, often conveyed in ways that a man is expected to understand.

For example, a vacationing husband and wife are driving on the freeway for several hours. The husband, unaware of subtext and indirect communication, only responds to the explicit and obvious.

After about 90 minutes of driving, the wife says, "Would you like to stop for some coffee?"

The husband, taking the statement literally, says, "No, let's keep going."

After another 30 minutes, the wife says, "Are you hungry? Maybe we should stop for some food."

The husband, intent on getting to the destination and again assuming the literal meaning of his wife's question, says, "No, I'm OK."

After another 45 minutes, the husband notices the wife does not respond to his conversation. She has an angry look, so he asks her what's wrong.

The wife suddenly blurts out, "I've been telling you for over an hour I have to go to the restroom!"

— Aesthetics

Young men with their own apartment tend to be pigs. They lack concern for aesthetic appearances, unaware that they are communicating something important and often uncomfortable to women.

Women often pay attention to living spaces and fashion precisely because they know that life is more than mere practicality.

One's living space and clothing express an inner state; one's being and consciousness.

Men can get so externally oriented that they don't take into account that internal state.

Women, on the other hand, tend to be much more aware and sensitive to inner states that are reflected in outer aesthetics.

Women therefore often strive to help "civilize" men by redecorating and dressing them.

Men should pay attention. It's important.

— Nonverbal behaviors, wholeness, and circularity.

Men who spend any time with women become aware that things are happening in women that just don't make sense to men. The problem is not necessarily with women.

> *Men have a responsibility to upgrade their awareness of nonverbal communication.*

Why do men have this responsibility? Is this a one-way street?

Since men tend to be explicit and direct, women do not have to work as hard figuring out men. Except to the extent that they believe men should read their minds and understand nonverbal cues.

Men are usually amateurs in subtext.

Women have a more holistic, indirect, and circular way of looking at the world.

For example, my wife had an event she was managing one Saturday afternoon. That morning I asked her, "What time does your event start?"

Male consciousness looks for a direct and simple response to that question.

Female consciousness hears a request for the whole picture.

So my wife began to tell a story…

"Well, at eleven o'clock I have to go get the signs out of storage, and then I meet up with my helpers at noon, and then…"

Knowing my wife and knowing how this works, I just started laughing.

She stopped and asked me, "What?"

And I said, "I just asked, 'What time does your event start?'"

She laughed and told me the time.

The wrong way to take what she did is apply the female stereotype that women just like to talk a lot. That's not what's happening.

Female consciousness operates differently, and men have to grow into the understanding of how that works.

Men can be lazy and dismiss female consciousness, rather than appreciate that it can often be more supple and subtle than male consciousness.

And therefore downright magnificent
and essential to a balanced, happy life.

Here's a story about how a woman faced a particularly unusual and challenging situation. This story is archived on the *This American Life* website. You can find it in the Prologue of episode 528: The Radio Drama Episode, broadcast on June 20, 2014.

https://tinyurl.com/sarvid4

Carin Gilfry makes her living by singing opera part time and recording audio books part time.

In 2013 she had a deadline for a children's book. Being in a hotel, she wanted to find a place to record that was quiet.

She has the tape recorder in the room, and decides to go into the hotel room closet and record, reading the book from her iPad into the tape recorder's microphone.

Shortly after starting, she wants to reset the tape recorder in the main room. She then realizes that she has locked herself in the closet. There was no way to unlock it from the inside.

And the tape recorder continues, recording her entire ordeal.

After a while, she realizes she has a bit of wireless access. So she tries dialing the front desk. She gets through, but the connection is so bad, she can't make the desk clerk understand her before it cuts out.

The recording continues with several minutes of silence, broken by her occasionally laughing desperately to herself.

She can't call her husband because he is in an audition with his phone off. She tries calling her mother, but there's no answer.

About 18 minutes after locking herself in, she hears a German couple in the hallway. She happens to speak German so she calls out for help. She hears them talking, but they walk away.

After a while, a housekeeper knocks, asking if she is OK.

The housekeeper finally lets her out 22 minutes after she had been locked in the closet.

She was terribly embarrassed about her situation. She wondered if she should give the housekeeper a tip.

She was approaching her situation primarily internally, working indirectly to free herself.

How would a typical male respond in the same situation?

Does anyone doubt what would happen?

Within ten minutes, a typical male would have broken down that door to get out of the closet. He would have blamed the hotel for constructing a closet that could lock someone in.

He would approached the situation externally, working directly to free himself.

By now you may be impatient with me, talking so much about men and women, as if they are the only ones to have relationships with each other.

Isn't life more complex than that?

Yes. Yet what I'm speaking to can easily translate into more specialized experiences.

I cannot address them all, but the next chapter lays down the essentials.

Chapter 7

Gay, Lesbian, Transgender, and the Rest

*Your state of consciousness
is your state of acceptance.*
Harold Klemp

Be strong.

Be honest.

Be loving.

And be true to yourself.

It doesn't matter who you love.
What matters is *that* you love.

Chapter 8

Romance, Part 1

*Romance is when someone you like walks into a room
and they take your breath away.
Romance is when two people are dancing
and they fit together perfectly.
Romance is when two people are walking next to each other
and all of a sudden they find themselves holding hands,
and they don't know how that happened.*
John C. Moffi

Romance is the lover at play.

An acquaintance of mine told me how he had asked his live-in partner to marry him.

He and his partner had lived together for several years. He had been married before and had grown children.

The kitchen faucet started acting up, so she got under the sink and began working on it. He was watching her work and was moved by how much he loved this remarkable person.

So he decided in that moment to ask her to marry him.

Her response?

"You ask me this...NOW?"

My acquaintance unknowingly violated the first rule of romance:

***Always make sure
your partner has a great story to tell.***

Here's how I asked my wife to marry me:

I had the ring, and I called up our best friends, two couples, Ed and Diane, and Paula and Bernard.

I explained that I was going to pop the question at an especially nice, upscale restaurant in Palo Alto, on a Sunday evening. The restaurant was in on it, and they had prepared two tables, one for me and my future wife, and a separate one that we would move to, set for six.

I wanted our friends to pick up six dozen sunflowers and six dozen roses that I had ready for them at a florist. Sunflowers were her favorite flower, and roses were for our love.

They would arrive at a predetermined time, about 15 minutes after we had sat down at the table. I would be positioned where I could see past her when they arrived with the flowers.

I played it cool that evening. I had told her we had reservations for dinner.

As the time approached, with her having worked that day (self-employed), she mentioned that she was not sure it was worth our dressing up.

I agreed that it might not be worth the effort, but I knew her. This restaurant was upscale just enough that business casual would work. But it was also a place where evening gowns and a coat and tie were appropriate.

After a while, she came back and said, "Why not dress up? It's a nice restaurant."

And, smiling inside, I agreed.

We arrived on time, the restaurant workers expectant, careful not to give anything away.

We relaxed and ordered drinks. Just on time, I saw our friends arrive carrying armfuls of flowers. She looked wide-eyed as they walked up smiling, holding the flowers in their arms.

Just then, I got up, dropped to one knee, held up a ring case, and opened it to reveal the ring.

A restaurant full of patrons and workers applauded.

The rest is history. And a darn good story.

Romance is about storytelling. Great and surprising stories. Unexpected stories.

All you need to do to be romantic is to create for your partner a great, living, unexpected, surprising story.

The wonderful thing about such stories is that the good ones get better in the telling. You will find that over time, as the story gets told over and over to others, that love is rekindled and romance stays in the air.

Don't fall into the trap of believing that the male in a relationship should be the prime story creator. Females have just as much an obligation to create stories for the men in their lives; stories you want them to tell their friends.

Never forget that your prime obligation in romance is very simple:

Create a great story.

Flirting

You've probably heard of the famous ancient Hindu text called the *Kama Sutra*. Contrary to popular belief, only a small portion of its 1250 verses in 36 chapters refers to actual sexual activity.

The *Kama Sutra* also details lessons on how to flirt and court someone:

Do you know the power of a coy gesture?

A furtive glance?

A slight, wry smile?

Do you understand the different kinds of smiles?

Do you realize that the eyes truly are the windows to the Soul?

That the looks you give, and the intent behind them, can indeed send darts?

Do you grasp how easily, though subconsciously, others will pick up your picture of yourself?

That you will radiate to others either a low or high opinion of yourself?

For those of you interested in learning how to flirt, the Kama Sutra may be too old-fashioned to be helpful. There are various modern guides to flirting, but they all boil down to a few basic rules.

1. Appearance matters. Sometimes being striking means being tasteful, not obvious.

2. The right smile can be properly suggestive. Again, be tasteful and restrained.

3. Easy laughter can go miles. Not joke telling, but appreciative laughter.

4. Capture with a look, but be restrained. Remember that less is more.

5. Know what you want and express an easy confidence.

6. Know how body language works. You may intend one thing while your body communicates something else. Make sure they are aligned.

Flirting works best when used sparingly, leaving the right amount of room for subtext.

You can take the example of the difference between good songs and great songs.

Good songs often apply to specific people and situations. For example, a love song may give someone's name, set the scene in a specific city, or provide some other limiting detail that is personal to the songwriter but not to many listeners.

A great song is more open. It lets the listener supply more personal meanings.

For example, some great songwriters will write a love song to their spiritual guru, but the language is so open that the listener will not realize who the target is. Listeners assume it's to a romantic love in the songwriter's life.

The words allow you to apply it to a lover, a child, anyone you can love. Listeners meet the song halfway and supply their own meanings.

The same is true with flirting. The more you can supply just enough anchor points to allow the person to supply the rest, the more intriguing you become.

Tell a story, explicitly and with subtext.
And let them supply part of the story.

Romance is always about playful storytelling. And playful storytelling provides the playground for love to blossom.

Love carves out new and often unknown territory.

Chapter 9

Love

*Sex is like washing your face—just
something you do because you have to.
Sex without love is absolutely ridiculous.
Sex follows love, it never precedes it.*
Sophia Loren

**The ancient Greeks have a word for everything; they had
four words for Love.**

In English we have essentially two: "love" and "like."

The French have one, *amore*, which can mean both "love" and "like."

Why would the Greeks have four words for love?

They loved making fine distinctions clearly in language. They had a rich and distinguishing vocabulary, which allowed them to be more specific than most languages.

They even had a word for the last stone left in the bottom of a bag.

You may have noticed the ancient Greek quote that I've put on every book in this series:

> *Make clear distinctions,*
> *and examine all things well.*
> The Golden Verses of Pythagoras

We explore the value of a rich and distinguishing vocabulary in *Language and Rhetoric: A Lifetime of Learning.*

Taking a cue from the Greeks, you can see the value of a rich and distinguishing vocabulary by examining their four words for the different kinds of love:

Eros: Physical love.

> Eros includes both sex and romance in the sense of sensual desire. It does not always mean the sex act itself. It may include a social element.

It's used to point to love that is more than the love of friendship (Philia).

Storge: Emotional love.

The closest English word is "affection," a natural affection like that of a parent for a child.

Philia: Mental love.

This is the love of friendship, as articulated by Aristotle. (We'll talk more about Aristotle in Chapters 10 and 12 as we explore love and happiness.) Philia includes loyalty to friends and family.

Agape: Spiritual love.

Agape refers to true unconditional love, a selfless love that does not require the one loved to return love. Some Christians will use this word for the unconditional love of God.

Understanding these four distinct kinds of love can help you sort out the different feelings you have for others. The lines between each are not hard and fast. They can blend.

In fact, when you are dating someone, you gain insight about the strength and nature of the relationship by seeing which of these loves are mutually shared.

Is the relationship based mainly in sensual feelings?

Can you say that a true friendship
and loyalty has developed?

Are selfless acts of love freely given?

I had an acquaintance that desired a man who would give her complete unconditional love. She was willing to give him unconditional love as well.

In fact, she had a written list of the things he had to do for her in order for her to give him unconditional love.

Act a certain way.

Give her specific kinds of gifts.

Take her on key vacations.

You see, her particular definition of "unconditional love" came with a list of conditions.

True unconditional love is probably the hardest kind of love to discover and attain. Society often does little to support it.

Why?

Because unconditional love is selfless in its service to another. Not self-negating, but self-sacrificing in the best sense. And persons giving it do not even think about what they are giving.

Unconditional love becomes part of their nature, not something self-referential.

Too many in society advertise their "unconditional love," turning it into something actually self-serving. (I support this noble cause! You should too!)

You recognize these people by the implicit moral superiority that exudes from their certainty. Those who truly exercise unconditional love are anonymous and have no patience for a spotlight on their love.

Great writers have attempted to explore different kinds of love and those needs that mask themselves as love.

Leo Tolstoy explores love in one of his greatest novels:

Anna Karenina explores two kinds of love portrayed side-by-side:

1) The love of the married Anna Karenina for the unmarried Count Vronsky. Both carry rank in the Russian social order.

2) The love of a country landowner, Konstantin, who seeks to marry the debutante Kitty. Kitty expects to make a fine social match, initially with Count Vronsky.

Some modern interpreters of Tolstoy's work would have us believe that Tolstoy is focused on portraying the outdated social order which fails to accept Anna's "modern" love, with Anna becoming a tragic heroine.

Not quite so. Tolstoy contrasts true unconditional love and the false love that plays out in social settings.

> The 2013 film *Anna Karenina*, written by Tom Stoppard, faithfully and brilliantly portrays Tolstoy's real purpose. Ultimately, Anna's is a self-indulgent Eros-based love that fails to reach Agape.
>
> At first the young Kitty, as expected by Anna and society, falls for the temporary societal definition of love. But she eventually realizes that Konstantin offers true unconditional love.
>
> The film smartly conveys the difference between artificial society and the naturalness outside society.
>
> When society and social customs dominate, all the characters are on stage playing their artificial parts.
>
> When they can be themselves, the settings are natural, in the open air, in the country.
>
> Anna tries to force society to change, to accept her natural feelings. Her mistake leads to her tragedy.
>
> The film ends with examples of Agape and of true unconditional love.

(See Appendix I for a couple of contrasting passages from *Anna Karenina*.]

Fyodor Dostoyevsky uses his great novel, *The Idiot,* to explore the question, *Could a naturally good person, one who gives unconditionally like a saint, survive in society?*

Young Prince Myshkin has spent a few years in a Swiss sanatorium. He comes home to Russia displaying an uncompromising gentle, giving, and trusting nature.

His behavior in society leads to disaster.

The novel ends leaving us wondering if someone like Prince Myshkin is fit only for a sanatorium.

Hence the title, *The Idiot.*

Shakespeare most famously portrays the difference between mere sex and true romance and unconditional love in *Romeo and Juliet.* (See Appendix I.)

Just before the famous balcony scene where Romeo, hidden in her garden, sees Juliet emerge, Shakespeare does something special.

Like placing a diamond on black velvet, he places the pure love and romance of the balcony scene on a black backdrop of a scene dripping with the raunchy sexual play of his friends.

Mercutio makes fun of Romeo's attraction to Juliet by comparing him and her (and all maids) to fruit that resembles sexual organs.

Then, after this bawdy sex-laced scene, Romeo says, "He jests at scars that never felt a wound," meaning that Mercutio, who has yet to experience love, makes fun of Romeo's love-scarred heart.

Romeo then turns and sees Juliet emerge, radiant like the sun at dawn. Although their story is tragic, Shakespeare's art is not.

The story of Romeo and Juliet is now almost a cliché, but a close reading discloses very real and illuminating distinctions between mere sexual lust and real love.

> *Nothing is more challenging than unconditional love, the kind of love that gives without any thought of receiving.*

Unconditional love is not dependent on sex or romance, or even marriage and commitment.

Unconditional love depends on nothing but itself.

That is not to say that unconditional love does not enhance sex, romance, marriage, and commitment. Indeed, at their best and most refined, sex, romance, marriage, and commitment embody unconditional love.

Imagine sex imbued with unconditional love.

Is there anything lustful or animalistic about such sex?

Is it actually elevating and sublime in its beauty?

Imagine romance imbued with unconditional love.

> Is there anything artificial or uncomfortable in those romantic advances and adventures?
>
> Is the experience more about sharing the wonder and joy of another?

Imagine marriage imbued with unconditional love.

> Is there ever a reason to hold anger or resentments, or to turn that person into a mere object of your pleasure?
>
> Would you ever fight with the person you love?
>
> Or does anger, resentments, and fighting signal areas of withholding, and a need to bring more unconditional love into your lives?

Imagine commitment imbued with unconditional love.

> Is there anything self-pitying about such a commitment?
>
> Would not such commitment embody loyalty, care, and joy experienced from the results of that commitment?

Unconditional love often develops most fully when one becomes a parent. Children often have a way of bringing adults out of themselves.

Parents will often sacrifice for the sake of their children's joy and partake of that joy.

Harold C. Goddard, a noted teacher of literature and writer about Shakespeare, gave a lecture in 1919 called *The Key to Walt Whitman*. (Published in a collection of essays called *The Alphabet of the Imagination*.)

In this lecture, he describes the essence of that key in the relationship between parent and child:

> When you were a very little boy, or girl, there used to come a time when there was just one chocolate cream left in the box. You wanted it dreadfully. But you were afraid, or perhaps you were too high-principled, to take it. So you just looked in at it, with a sigh.
>
> And then, quite to your surprise, you heard your mother saying, "Take it, my dear," in a tone that seemed to add, "It will give me more pleasure to have you eat it than to eat it myself."

Goddard notes how a child would wonder why a parent would do such a thing. But then the child one day grows up and becomes a parent.

> You looked out the window one morning and saw your little girl strutting proudly off in her new coat. Or you saw your little boy riding past on his new bicycle.
>
> And a revelation of exactly how that youngster was feeling came over you so

intensely that for an instant you could hardly have told whether you were indoors or out, whether you were yourself or that child.

Somewhere a barrier had broken down. Somehow you realized, as a solid fact, what you had hitherto always considered sentimental pretense: that it is possible to have as much fun out of someone else's fun as out of your own.

...[T]hat coat and that bicycle were among the best investments you ever made. The paradox of your mother and the chocolate cream was explained.

That is an experience of unconditional love.

And unconditional love then provides the key to bringing more joy into your life through gift-giving.

Think about Christmas or birthdays, or some other occasion where you received the perfect gift.

Do you remember the joy you felt?

Now think of the time you gave someone you cared about the perfect gift.

Do you remember the joy you felt?

Here is a secret to life and joy:

*The joy you experience
receiving the perfect gift
is the same as
the joy you experience
giving the perfect gift.*

The question then becomes:

Which action do you have the most control over?

Getting the perfect gift or giving one?

**Giving without any thought of receiving
is the secret to constant joy.
And the essence of unconditional love.**

Chapter 10

Marriage

A successful marriage requires falling in love many times,
always with the same person.
Mignon McLaughlin

Marriage is a powerful rite of passage.

The first book in this series, *Creating Your Life: A Lifetime of Learning*, describes how powerful it can be.

Here's an excerpt from that section:

> Often, people improve with the change in picture.
> Their hearts open wide, they become more giving,
> and they step into the best picture of themselves.
> Friends and acquaintances begin to see the newly
> married, no longer as mere separate individuals, but
> as a couple who embody unconditional love.
>
> But marriage can go in the other direction.
> Sometimes people go through profound personality
> changes when they marry. A whole new picture
> takes hold, because they "know" that this is how a
> "married person" is supposed to act.
>
> Think about it.
>
> Before getting married, two people walk around
> thinking of themselves as single, being single, acting
> single. Then they go before a powerful authority
> who declares, "Now you are married; go out and live
> it" and PRANG! They go out and live it.
>
> They think of themselves as married, being married,
> acting married.
>
> What really changes? Nothing but the PICTURE
> they hold of themselves. The picture changes.
> Nothing else happens.
>
> Sometimes people go through profound personality
> changes when they marry. A whole new picture
> takes hold, because they "know" that this is how a
> "married person" is supposed to act.

Men who seemed sweet and reasonable and shared household burdens suddenly demand that their new "wife" do all the cooking, cleaning, and laundry.

Women suddenly expect their new "husband" to take on the "natural" role of handyman and protector.

Many people marry for the wrong reasons and end up single, often with obligations, and holding a cynical view of love and relationships.

But a short, simple test can help guide you toward what a successful marriage may look like.

The Four Marriage Questions

If you and your potential spouse can both answer "yes" to most or all four of these questions, then you may end up with a great marriage.

Of course, there are no guarantees. Life always has a way of surprising us.

Ask yourself each question. Can you say yes to each?

1) If this person stays just as he or she is for the rest of his or her life, would that be OK?

2) Would you like to become more like this person?

3) If you were to have a child with someone, would you want to have a child with this person?

4) If the child grew up to be exactly like this person, would that be OK?

It's a simple test.

You may consider memorizing these four questions and share them with everyone you know.

I once got a call from my wife. She was at the home of a friend whose daughter was going to be married in one week to her high school sweetheart.

She was visiting her mother, crying and upset, unsure whether the marriage was a good idea.

Four weeks before, he had called off the wedding. She was devastated and gave back the ring. He had come back to her the next day, sobbing, begging her to come back and get married.

They travelled to Las Vegas, but did not get married. When they returned, she had called off the wedding. Her friends gave her mixed messages about whether marrying him was a good idea.

She told her mother that she had felt like she had to go through with it because her parents had spent so much money. But she learned they didn't care about that.

My wife called me and asked, "What are those four marriage questions again?"

I gave them to her, and she asked the daughter each question. The daughter answered "no" to all four.

She cancelled the wedding, and in two years she married a wonderful man. And they now have three beautiful children.

The four marriage questions may help you recognize that a potential partner may not be the best fit. They hint at what is required of your character.

This is not a book of advice on making a marriage work. Like so many things in life, each marriage has a special set of characteristics that make it unlike almost any other. Plenty has been written on marriage by academics and self-help experts of all kinds.

Many of them have not experienced a long-lasting happy marriage.

But I will suggest that if you take into account what the rest of this book has to offer, you are more likely to discover what makes a fine marriage.

In the meantime, I'll offer one critical aspect of marriage: Friendship.

Friendship

In his Nichomachean Ethics, Aristotle distinguishes roughly three kinds of friendship:

1) Those based on pleasure.

2) Those based on usefulness.

3) Those based on themselves.

We all have experienced friendships based on pleasure.

These are the friends that are fun to hang with. We go to parties with these kinds of friends. We play fun games with these kinds of friends. We enjoy sex with these kinds of friends.

These are the partiers, the gamers, the friends with benefits. And we also know a critical truth about these kinds of friendships:

> *For friendships based on pleasure,*
> *once the pleasure ends,*
> *the friendship ends.*

When we no longer party in the same way, or play the same games, or we lose interest in the sex, more often than not, these friendships end.

Why?

Because the primary purpose of the friendship has ended—its pleasure.

These friendships are not necessarily bad. They can help people learn and grow, and pass the time. But rightly or wrongly:

> *Friendships based on pleasure*
> *are means to an end,*
> *not an end in themselves.*

We all have also experienced friendships based on usefulness.

These are the friends we have at the office or at work. These are the friends at school. These are friends who show up at our political rallies. These are friends at the club or the association or the church where we go.

They are our coworkers, our classmates, our political allies, and our fellow club members. They are useful friendships. As long as we have common goals, related to work or politics or mutual aims, the friendship endures.

And we also know a critical truth about these kinds of friendships:

> *Friendships based on usefulness*
> *are means to an end,*
> *not an end in themselves.*

Once the usefulness ends, the friendship ends.

Once we change our job or political party or religion, we may say we want to keep in touch. Perhaps we do occasionally meet and have lunch together.

But more often than not, the friendship ends.

Why?

Because the primary purpose of this friendship has ended—its usefulness.

Then there is the third kind of friendship, the friendship based on itself.

Some people can go their whole lives without experiencing this kind of friendship. These friendships are rare. These are the friends who, if you have them, you usually can count the number of them on one hand.

These are the friends who you just enjoy being with, and they enjoy being with you. It does not matter what you are doing, nor how pleasurable or useful it is to be together. You just feel good being with them.

These are the friends who, sometimes, you don't see for years. And then when you are together again, it's like no time has passed. You are right there together again.

Nothing useful or specifically pleasurable comes out of these kinds of friendships. They promise no previous obligation or future benefit.

They just *are*.

> *Friendships based on themselves*
> *are not means to an end,*
> *They are ends in themselves.*

These are the friends that are never lost with changing jobs, locations, pleasures, or pains.

These friendships are timeless.

Marriages Based on the Three Kinds of Friendships

Understanding the kinds of friendships helps us understand the kinds of marriages.

> *Imagine you married based on pleasure.*

You've found a fun and exciting person. Life with this person is like a party. The travel is great, the conversation is great, and the sex is great.

You get married.

And after a few months, or a few years, the party ends. Sure, some of the fun still happens. Occasionally. But life is no longer a constant party.

As the pleasure winds down, the marriage winds down. And either you live a life together as acquaintances instead of friends, just getting through the day, or staying together for the kids; or your marriage ends.

Imagine you married based on usefulness.

You wanted a life of money and leisure, so you married. You can afford to travel, associate with rich friends, dress in designer clothes, and go to the best parties.

But then your spouse loses everything in the stock market.

Does the marriage last?

You wanted someone as beautiful as a model as a spouse, someone who you can display like a trophy. Someone whom you show off at a party or a political event. People think well of you because you attracted such a person into your life.

But then your spouse is disfigured in an auto accident and now requires a wheelchair.

Does the marriage last?

When the marriage is a means to an end,
you risk the marriage ending
when the reason for the marriage ends.

Sometimes a marriage based on pleasure that results in children turns into a marriage based on usefulness—the children need a family, so a couple stays together out of a sense of usefulness to the children.

Now imagine a marriage based on itself.

Pleasures can come and go. Usefulness can come and go. But neither becomes the foundation for the marriage.

A marriage can be based on itself,
and ideally includes pleasures and usefulness.

Pleasure can mean sex together, travel together, conversation together, movies or music together. Or any other of a number of pleasurable things a couple can do together.

Usefulness can mean working together, creating a home together, supporting each other, learning from each other, raising a family together, contributing to the community together. Or any other of a number of useful things a couple can do together.

But the marriage is not based on any of these. The pleasure and usefulness becomes the furniture that fills out a house created out of the friendship itself.

A marriage founded on a friendship based on itself requires, at its core, two simple yet challenging behaviors:

Kindness and generosity.

A psychologist, John Gottman, conducted research tracking thousands of married couples of many years. He

divided them into two major groups: the masters and the disasters.

The masters cultivated a culture of love and intimacy largely absent from the disasters.

> *The masters practiced kindness*
> *and generosity daily in their lives.*

> *The disasters brought contempt,*
> *criticism, and hostility.*

Gottman could predict with 94% certainty whether couples (poor or rich, straight or gay, with children or without) would be happily together years later, or would be unhappy or divorced.

And the number one factor that tore marriages apart?

Contempt.

In short, meanness kills marriage.

Kindness and generosity nourishes a marriage. Such is the core of a friendship based on itself. And a marriage based on itself, in the right kind of friendship, opens a new world.

> *For a fine marriage balances and embodies*
> *an understanding of sex and romance,*
> *male and female consciousness,*
> *and love, and friendship,*
> *and generosity, and kindness.*

One important point: The marriage does not mean the end of romance. Romance can manifest itself in new ways.

Chapter 11

Romance, Part 2

Marriage: Love is the reason.
Lifelong friendship is the gift.
Kindness is the cause.
Til' death do us part is the length...
A great spouse loves you exactly as you are.
An extraordinary spouse helps you grow;
inspires you to be, do and give your very best.
Fawn Weaver

If romance ends with marriage, then the marriage is likely to end as well.

Romance in marriage is still the lover at play, but in new and different ways.

Perhaps the poems and letters have come to an end, which is understandable when a couple are wooing each other at a distance.

Being apart breeds desire for connection.

But other opportunities arrive when a couple is together and committed.

> *The ways of romance at a distance*
> *transform when the distance is measured*
> *in feet or inches rather than miles.*

Many ways exist to frame romance after commitment. In his book *The Five Love Languages*, Gary Chapman offers an interesting and compelling framework:

1) Words of Affirmation.

2) Quality Time.

3) Receiving Gifts.

4) Acts of Service.

5) Physical Touch.

His book is worth reading if you want stories about, and good suggestions for increasing, the verbal and nonverbal love languages.

I will reapply his framework in terms of romance after commitment. And please keep in mind that all of these languages have overlaps. For example, all can be seen as gifts as well as acts of service.

Words of Affirmation

As you'll recall from *Creating Your Life: A Lifetime of Learning*, the language we use often has the power to create. What we affirm about ourselves can influence who we become.

> *We move toward and become like what we put our attention on.*

And what we affirm about others influences the picture they hold of themselves, especially if they grant us that influence.

Remember the Pygmalion Effect?

> In 1968, a study was done by two researchers, **Rosenthal and Jacobson,** which demonstrated what they called the "Pygmalion Effect."
>
> They told teachers that the researchers would test the intelligence of children aged six to twelve years, all drawn from the same school. They then

randomly assigned children to two groups.

Their teachers were told that the children in one group were "high achievers" even though they were randomly chosen. At the end of the school year, these children showed significant test gains, despite the random allocation to a group.

In short, the researchers discovered that the teachers' expectations manifested in the children.

> *We can uncritically accept subconsciously pictures other people hold of us.*

So imagine how powerful our words can be to our beloved, who is close to us every day. (I love the word *beloved*. Let's commit to bringing it back into style.)

Are your words loving, inspiring, and motivating? Or do they tend more often to be critical or even contemptuous?

Do your words reflect that you both love *and* like your beloved? Or do they create a feeling with your beloved of having to walk on eggshells that could break with a single misstep?

Romance is now a repetitive and continuous series of actions. It's what you do every day, every week, every month, every year.

And the words you use
either build or destroy.

Romance builds. The end of romance shows up as words of destruction.

So, if you do not believe you have enough romance in your life, your first step is to look at your language. Especially look to how you talk about your beloved to others.

Do you, more often than not, deny your beloved? ("You're wrong. You aren't capable of doing that.")

Or do you, more often than not, affirm your beloved? ("It may be a challenge, but I think you're up to it. Give it a try.")

The goal is simple:

First make sure you affirm
at least 90% of the time;
and then work to make that 100%.

Quality Time

— Do you actively listen to your beloved?

— Do you maintain eye contact and respond thoughtfully?

— Do you and your beloved engage in regular activities together?

— Do you share pleasures?

In other words, do you share and schedule quality time together?

One way my wife and I keep romance alive appears to be a simple non-romantic tradition, but we see it as romantic.

Every Saturday morning, we go out to breakfast together to one of our favorite little breakfast spots. We often talk and read together while we're there.

Sometimes, we meet other regular couples and share some conversation.

It's regular quality time together, and only extraordinary events bump it from our schedule.

That's a weekly activity. However, we also share activities that sometimes come around months or even years apart.

> One of our long-term shared activates is traveling to Europe.

> We spent our honeymoon in England and Ireland.

> A few years later we spent Christmas in Florence, Italy.

We spent our ten-year anniversary in Vienna, Austria, going to operas and palace festivals with dancing.

And a few years later, we spent a month traveling through other parts of northern and central Italy.

We discovered on our honeymoon that we both travel well together. We like similar ways of scheduling our travel. Our travel rhythms and interests are wonderfully aligned.

So we've made travel to Europe one of our traditions, a romantic ritual of spending quality time together. We save our money and plan our time so we can sustain what we love to do together...

No matter how many years come between trips.

Romance means quality traditions, repeated activities that you love doing together.

Receiving Gifts

Gifts of love come in many forms: words of affirmation, quality time, and material gifts of all shapes and sizes...

Even Gifts of Self qualify; that is, gifts of your time, your attention, your positive presence.

Gifts fit into the idea of quality traditions, planned activities that arrive periodically. Birthdays and anniversaries are the most common. The trick is, can you make them uncommon and special?

> Once I had a new girlfriend. One Valentine's Day, I went to FAO Schwarz in San Francisco. I found a huge stuffed animal, a cute St. Bernard almost as big as I was.
>
> I then bought a dozen red roses.
>
> I was walking down a street near Union Square carrying the St. Bernard over my left shoulder and holding the dozen roses in my right hand.
>
> A woman walked up to me, smiled, and said, "I'm going to go home and slap my boyfriend!"
>
> I won the girl. The St. Bernard now lies near our front door with a little puppy St. Bernard resting on his back.

In our home we have birthday months (and for some of our dearest relatives, we have birthday years.)

Why?

> *Simple. The best gifts never come with a sense of duty.*

When you target a specific date, you can easily fall into the trap of getting a last-minute gift for the date rather than the appropriate gift that reflects the nature of your beloved.

So my wife gets a birthday month. I can provide one or more gifts during that month. It may take a number of forms, but the month gives me plenty of time to find or "discover" something just right.

For example, one year my wife, a semi-professional photographer, started taking pictures of owls. Owls started showing up around the home. I started thinking that we were living in Hogwarts.

I knew from previous experience with dragonflies, butterflies, and hummingbirds, that once they start showing up in one place, they start showing up in all kinds of ways.

So I began searching for gifts related to owls, not knowing what I might discover. (In the language of *Creating Your Life*, I opened up my Reticular Activating System.)

I knew she loved unusual watches, so I started looking for watches with owls. I searched online stores for a couple of days until I found a good one.

I also went to a women's clothing department store, knowing she liked cashmere, and wondering if there could be a cashmere sweater with an owl on it.

I did not find one, but I asked several women in different departments if they had seen *any* clothing with an owl on it. Finally, one said yes and pointed me in the right direction.

I found a great little top that was just her size, the only piece of clothing in the entire store that had an owl on it.

That was a good birthday month!

Thoughtful gifts require some creative effort and time. And given enough time with creative effort, you often make unintended discoveries of fun combinations of gifts.

(One year I gave her a different birthday card on every day of her birthday month.)

Sometimes gifts are as simple as contacting a few close friends and arranging a small birthday lunch or dinner.

Other times, they can be as simple as giving your beloved three fun choices: a night at the theater, a weekend getaway, or a simple act of cooking a meal.

And remember:

*Often, the best gifts surprise your beloved,
because they are random, out of the blue,
and not connected to any special day.*

Acts of Service

Couples easily fall into routines, where one or the other is expected to own certain tasks.

One may be expected to manage lawn care, handle vehicle maintenance, take out the garbage, and fix the computer. The other may be expected to cook the meals, care for the baby, clean the bathrooms, and do the laundry.

Romance seeks ways to occasionally surprise and relieve your beloved of a routine through an act of service. Acts of service offer the Gift of Self. And one way to give this gift is to take on something routine (or hire someone) so your beloved can rest, play, or in some way replace the routine with some quality time.

What can you say to your beloved to break up a routine?

1) "No, let me cook tonight" or "Let's go to a restaurant tonight and let someone else cook."

2) "Let me change the diapers today."

3) "How about we hire someone to clean the house once or twice a month?"

There are plenty of routines. Watch your beloved and wonder to yourself, "How can I help?"

One more thought about acts of service: Is there anything your beloved has repeatedly asked you to do that you have not yet done?

> *Listen to your beloved:*
> *He or she is constantly*
> *asking you for gifts of service.*

Physical Touch

Connie Podesta is a motivational keynote speaker. You can find a variety of funny and insightful video clips of her on YouTube.

https://tinyurl.com/sarvid5

In one of her recorded talks, she talks about difficult people. She makes the case that difficult people don't feel loved. She tells a fascinating story about a man named Harold:

> A small hospital invited Connie to speak at a mandatory all-employee meeting. As you can imagine, nothing makes employees happier than a mandatory meeting.
>
> In the back sat Harold. He looked like he was ready for retirement.

He slouched in his chair, arms folded, giving her a look that said, "I hate being here. There's nothing you have to offer me."

Wanting to include him, Connie went up and asked him his name. He replied that he didn't have to tell her. He was present, and that's all that was required.

She found a couple of other people in the audience more responsive. At break time, people came up to her and told her about old, mean Harold.

They said he'd been like this for five years. He used to be nice, but now he was nasty and mad, so people avoided him.

They didn't know what had happened, but nobody talked to him anymore or invited him to anything.

When the session started again, she walked up to Harold, sat in his lap, and continued delivering her talk.

After three minutes, she started to get up, but he pulled her back into his lap. She talked that way for 45 minutes and at the end, his head lay on her shoulder.

After the session, she followed him out and asked him if he was OK. He turned to her sobbing, came up to her, and put his arms around her.

He said, "You are the first person who has touched me since my wife died, five years ago."

We underestimate the power of touch.

How often do you touch your beloved? With a hug, a kiss, something more intimate?

Do you do it daily, first thing in the morning, last thing in the evening?

Or can days or weeks go by without a hug, a touch on the art, a stroke on the hair, holding hands, a brush of the neck, kisses lightly around the eyes and on the cheeks, little massages on the back, or touching of feet?

Touch expresses intimacy.

Touch is the gift of service
that affirms quality.

Chapter 12

Happiness

It's your right to know joy.
Leo Buscaglia

If the government were to offer you a free daily Happy Pill, would you take it?

*A pill that would
remove all your worries,
relieve all your pain,
eliminate any possible suffering?*

Would you take it?

And would you call yourself a happy person while on that pill?

If you are like most healthy people, you have an instinctive reaction against the idea of a Happy Pill.

Why?

Is it because you feel:

> — Like you're being controlled?

> — That you are losing something valuable and essential?

> — You're somehow no longer a real human being if you take it?

> — That your life would be more that of an animal or plant than a human being?

Many people look at all the pain and suffering in the world, and they want it to stop. They want everyone to be happy. And they believe everyone *should* be happy; otherwise, life is not fair.

Therefore, the Happy Pill would be a good thing, right?

No more pain, no more suffering.

The idea of a Happy Pill assumes something significant:

> — That pain and suffering have no purpose, no value.

— That pain and suffering have nothing to contribute to a happy life.

— That a world without pain and suffering would be a better world.

Think about such a Happy-Pill world:

No one would find anything painful.

No one would know they made a mistake.

No one would know when they took a false step.

No one would feel the need to empathize with the pain of others, since no one would be in pain.

No one would need to grow or change.

No one would need to feel compassion for anyone else.

Everyone would be equal. Everyone would feel the same happiness.

> *Everyone would be in their*
> *own little happy world*
> *with other people all equally*
> *in their own little happy worlds.*

And we all know how important it is for all people to be equal, right?

Does this Happy Pill world sound like a real life to you?

Is this *really* the kind of world you want to live in?

What is Happiness?

Figuring out the definition of something often means comparing it to, and contrasting it with, other things to see how it is different.

Is happiness the same thing as contentment or satisfaction or pleasure?

Or are they all different things?

Let's compare and contrast each of these to happiness:

> *Can you be satisfied and not be happy?*

> *Can you be content and not be happy?*

> *Can you experience pleasure and still not be happy?*

Another way to explore the question of happiness is to ask…

> *Can someone be struggling or suffering hardships, yet still be happy?*

The answer to these four questions should be "yes" for anyone who thinks them through.

Yes, you can be satisfied but not happy.

> You have heard of people who have made all the money they need, but end up killing themselves.

Yes, you can be content but not happy.

Like being satisfied, being content is a small state of consciousness.

You've just made a good bargain, perhaps buying something valuable for a price far below what it is worth. You are content.

But does that feel like happiness?

Doesn't happiness feel like it should be something larger?

Yes, you can experience pleasure and not be happy.

You just ate a good meal, heard good music, or experienced great sex.

Does that mean you are happy?

Does the pleasure stay or go away over time?

Isn't there something about happiness that is more...permanent?

Yes, you can struggle and suffer hardships and still be happy.

Talk to parents who have successfully raised children who have gone on to successfully raise their own children.

They may have suffered and experienced loss, yet they see that they have had a complete life. Despite the struggles, they are happy.

Why?

Exactly what is happiness? That is, true happiness, not anyone's relative, momentary personal opinion of happiness?

Is it possible to define this kind of happiness?

A Short History of Happiness

The ancient Greek philosophers, Plato and Aristotle, had different, though related, definitions of happiness.

Plato, in the *Euthydemus*, acknowledges that happiness seems to rely on acquiring good things. But in the *Symposium,* he makes clear that a balance is involved:

> *Happiness is spiritual well-being.*
> *A harmony in the Soul,*
> *an inner peace arising from*
> *a proper order of all parts of the Soul.*

In *The Republic,* Plato goes so far as to say that a happy person would receive an injustice rather than inflict an injustice on another.

In Plato's world, a happy person would never forcibly rule over another.

Aristotle, in his *Nichomachean Ethics*, provides another angle on the definition of happiness:

> *Happiness is living a complete life;*
> *the ultimate purpose of life being*
> *an activity achieved by exercising*
> *positive virtues, even in difficult situations.*

It is a life of purpose and noble achievements, even when recognized by no one but the happy person.

Those virtues, according to Aristotle, include Courage, Generosity, Justice, Friendship, and Citizenship.

There are hundreds of books on happiness. But it seems that many of today's writers have little to add to Aristotle.

Perhaps the key to Aristotle is to understand what he implies but never directly states, at least in modern terms. But we will get to that at the end of this chapter.

Dennis Prager, in his book, *Happiness is a Serious Problem*, believes that happiness cannot be defined for everyone. However, he does think that achieving happiness in its full form requires wisdom, and the hard work and self-discipline to put that wisdom into practice.

You can get an idea where he aims the reader by some of his chapter titles:

"Happiness is a Moral Obligation"

"Unhappiness is Easy—Happiness Takes Work"

"Comparing Ourselves with Others"

"Equating Happiness with Success"

"Equating Happiness with Fun"

"Seeing Yourself as a Victim"

"Develop a Perspective: Cultivate a Philosophy of Life"

"Life is Tragic"

"Find the Positive"

"Accept Tension"

"Everything has a Price—Know What It Is"

"Seek to Do Good"

"Find and Make Friends"

His chapter on friendship is particularly interesting, with subtitles like "Family," "Marriage," "Finding Friends," and "Keeping Friends." Aristotle's definitions of friendship can be seen implied in this chapter.

Charles Murray has written a wonderful little book: *The Curmudgeon's Guide to Getting Ahead: Dos and Don'ts of Right Behavior, Tough Thinking, Clear Writing, and Living a Good Life.*

This book is a must for young people looking to make their way into the working world.

Here's a glimpse of the kind of profound, solid advice he gives to the youth. Although he offers this advice in a chapter other than that on Happiness, it applies to anyone seeking happiness:

> You probably possess two of the most important personal qualities for success—high cognitive ability and good interpersonal skills. But it is unlikely that you have already developed another important trait: resilience.

Murray provides the dictionary definition of resilience as the ability of a material to return to its original shape after being stretched or deformed in some way.

Young people who have not exercised their capacity to be resilient are more like crystal glasses. But they have the potential to exercise resilience and learn to bounce back like a Super Ball.

He continues:

> ... if you've grown up in a loving and untroubled environment, that potential is unrealized. Here's the problem: You can be sure that your resilience will be tested sooner or later. When it happens, you don't want to shatter into glittering shards. If my description fits you, now is the time, when you're still single and more or less without responsibilities, to start exercising your elastic limit.

Such character traits as resilience, tenacity, focus, independence, self-reliance, and many more need exercise to develop.

> *Good parents, teachers, and friends*
> *actively help you build these character traits.*

Each of these character traits has a role to play in a life that can truly be called happy.

In the section Murray titles "On the Pursuit of Happiness," he provides some advice that hits true (built right on Aristotle's definition of happiness: *"lasting and justified satisfaction with life as a whole."*)

He develops six ideas. Check out his book to appreciate how he eloquently develops each idea:

1) Show up.

2) Take the clichés about fame and fortune seriously.

3) Take religion seriously, especially if you've been socialized not to. (Murray describes himself as agnostic.)

4) Take the clichés about marriage seriously.

5) Be open to a startup marriage instead of a merger marriage.

6) Watch *Groundhog Day* repeatedly.

If you have never seen the movie *Groundhog Day* with Bill Murray, put it at the top of your movie list and watch it as soon as you finish this book.

Hugh Hewitt, who teaches constitutional law, frames his book *The Happiest Life* around gifts and givers. For him, generosity is the precondition for happiness.

He first works his way through "The Seven Gifts": *Encouragement, Energy, Enthusiasm, Empathy, Good Humor, Graciousness, and Gratitude.*

Of these seven gifts, he says:

Everyone is eligible to be a giver of these gifts. Everyone. You don't need wealth. You don't have to be twenty-one. You don't even have to be literate.

And if you're not giving these away, you are being a miser.

Then he follows with the seven kinds of givers we can be:

> *The Spouse, The Parent, Family Members, Friends, The Coworker, Teachers, and The Church.*

And to be a giver, you not only need to have generosity, but also courage. He starts the introduction of the book with a quote from the ancient Greek General, Thucydides:

> *The secret of happiness is freedom, and the secret of freedom is courage.*

Hewitt then writes:

> You have to have courage to give away what you hold dearest, again and again and again. Every day. Remarkably, self-sacrifice and generosity produce the greatest, most enduring happiness.

Hewitt's book is warm and wise, and full of illustrative stories to provide a sharp and insightful definition of the gifts.

For example, to bring home what *empathy* actually is (as opposed to *sympathy*), he shares a conversation he had with a rabbi.

> *Sympathy is sharing suffering at a distance. Empathy is sharing suffering up close.*

The rabbi said simply, "Show up and shut up."

You don't have to tell the suffering person that you know what they're going through. You don't know.

You don't have to tell them it will be all right. You don't have to share your own experience with suffering.

As Hewitt says, "The gift of quiet, advice-free companionship in the midst of suffering is a gift of the highest order."

He makes the point that empathy is a costly gift because it means "reliving past sorrows and entering into new ones."

Balance

Why so much talk of happiness in a book about sex and romance?

Simple: We seek sex and romance, not as ends in themselves, but as means to happiness. And often, thinking sex and romance are central to happiness, we discover they are only the beginning.

Although happiness is composed of many parts, knowing those parts and seeking a balance among them may help you move closer to happiness.

And that brings us to the Balance Wheel.

Most balance wheels have from eight to twelve spokes. The idea is that the center of the wheel represents 0 and the outer edge represents 10. On this scale, 0 equals unfulfilled and 10 equals completely fulfilled.

Once you fill out your wheel and connect the spokes, you find how well it rolls, how bumpy it is, and where you may need to focus your efforts.

Here's an example of a balance wheel:

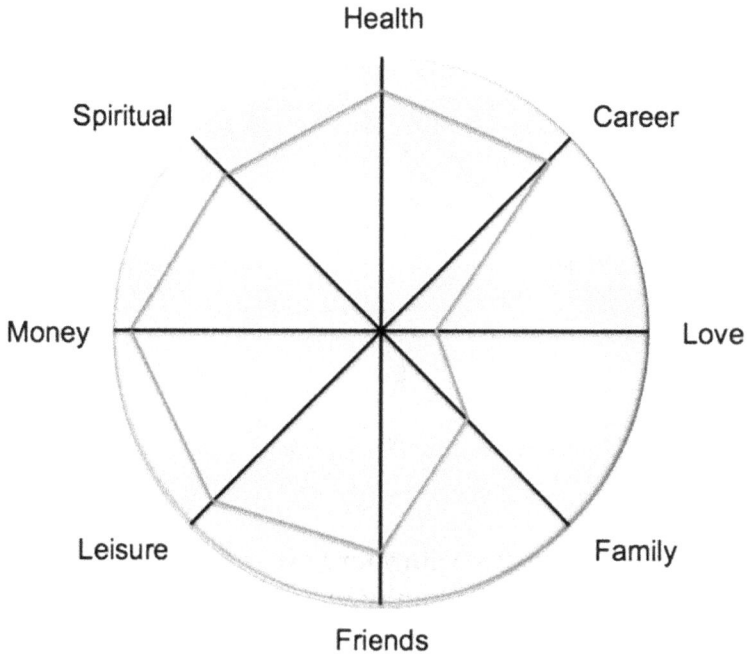

This wheel obviously runs rough, given the big chink in Love and Family. By working on these two, the wheel acquires some balance for a person seeking happiness.

Here's another way to frame the wheel:

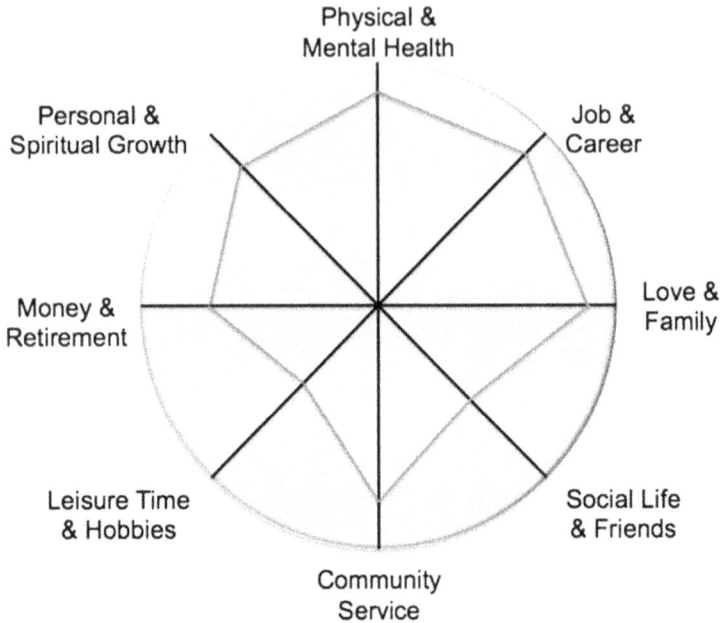

This wheel shows how there may be a necessary trade-off.

If you are satisfied with your Love & Family, as well as with your level of Community Service, you may find that your choices affect how much Leisure Time and Hobbies you can prioritize. Perhaps Community Service qualifies as what you do with your Leisure Time.

In any event, try constructing your balance wheel, and select the topics that are a high priority in your life. See if the gaps in the wheel make sense, and whether you should shift some of your creative energy into developing them.

Remember what you learned in *Creating Your Life: A Lifetime of Learning*. You can bring some greater balance to your life and move towards creating more the life you want.

But you have to know where to focus your energy and how to properly set goals.

And you need to patiently work through your blind spots, and any subconscious pictures that hold you back.

Then you have a shot at experiencing true joy in your life.

The Key to Happiness

Here is my personal balance wheel as of June 2014:

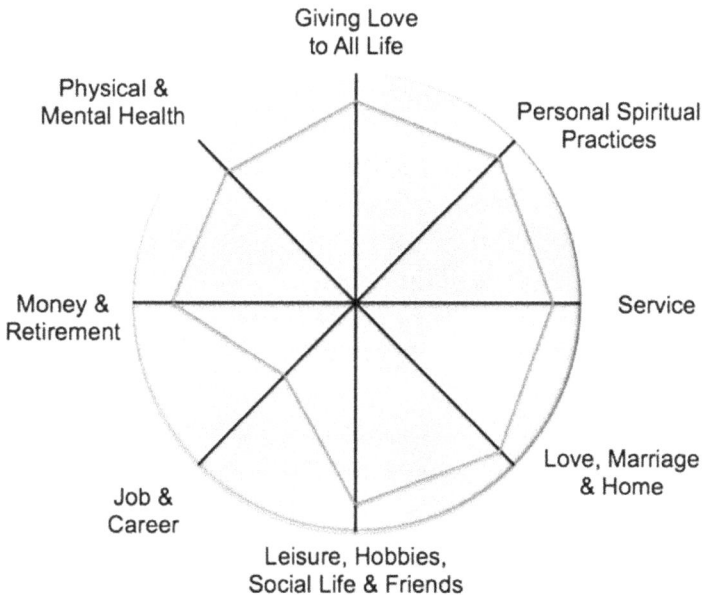

As you can see, all are fairly balanced, except for my job and career, which is in transition. My job role has shifted after a merger in the Silicon Valley company, where I work. My future there is uncertain, and I'm not sure how well I will take to the new role.

What is the best thing for me to do?

Focus on my job and career, and have contingency plans in place to manage every possible transition, whether within or without that company.

However, I have little to complain about. Since much of my life in other areas is doing so well, I am in a strong position to manage the gap in my wheel.

Why are they doing so well? Notice what I prioritize, how many of the spokes on the wheel have to do with love and service and spiritual practices and friends.

The secret, for me, has to do with working hard, daily, on giving unconditional love.

No matter what your spiritual orientation (including atheism or agnosticism), Paul Twitchell, in his poetic book, *Stranger by the River,* in a chapter simply called "Love," captures the essence of this idea:

> The requirements of growth demand that you exert the greatest degree of love for what is perfectly in accord with Soul. Our highest happiness will be best attained through our understanding of, and conscious cooperation with, the divine law.
>
> It is love that imparts vitality to our minds and hearts and enables it to germinate. The law of love will bring to you all necessity for your spiritual growth and maturity.
>
> Therefore, if you desire love, try to realize that the only way to get love is by giving love. That the more you give, the more you get; and the only way in

which you can give is to fill yourself with it, until you become a magnet of love.

Look at your life right now:

— Do you have enough joy in your life?

— Do you have enough unconditional love?

— Are you ready to make the changes necessary to get more joy and love into your life?

— Are you ready to do the hard work of transforming yourself into a different kind of person?

Well, now you know the secret. Now you know what you need to be doing every day of your life, from this point on, no matter what.

And no matter how hard it is initially.

And as you give without any thought of receiving, as you allow such giving to take over more and more of your life, you will begin to see the greatest secret of all.

The great secret hidden within all the most holiest and sacred of places throughout history.

The secret that no one can explain or give to another.

The secret that has always been hiding itself in plain sight within your secret heart.

You Gain All by Giving All.

THE *SEX AND ROMANCE* CHECKLIST

Love is always bestowed as a gift—
freely, willingly, and without expectation.
We don't love to be loved, we love to love.
Leo Buscaglia

BE AWARE OF THE INTOXICATING POWER OF SEX.

__ Sexual energy diminishes your judgment like alcohol.

__ Be wary of anyone attempting to stimulate your sexual energy; they know that with sexual energy, they can change your No to a Yes.

__ Pornography can be intoxicating, but it is, by its nature, animalistic and demeaning.

__ Severe overindulgence in sex can have harmful physical and psychological effects.

__ Girls can manipulate boys with sexual intoxication, just as boys attempt to manipulate girls with it.

UNDERSTAND HOW BOYS AND GIRLS EXPERIENCE SEXUAL ENERGY DIFFERENTLY.

__ For girls, sex is often a profound *emotional and internal* experience.

__ For boys, sex is primarily a *physical and external* experience.

__ While girls can carry intimate feelings after sex, boys after sex can easily forget about a girl and her feelings.

__ If a girl wants a boy to understand what she wants to get out of sex, she has to explicitly tell him.

__ Boys rarely have the maturity to handle a girl getting pregnant.

__ Even "good" boys will take advantage of girls who get drunk at parties.

__ Boys never care about a girl more just because she gives him sex.

__ Some boys make bets about taking a girl's virginity.

__ Older men can still be boys inside, even though they seem more mature.

RECOGNIZE THE DIFFERENCES BETWEEN MALE AND FEMALE CONSCIOUSNESS.

__ Men find joy in external activities, and often talk about things outside themselves.

__ Women find joy in internal states, and often talk about things inside themselves.

__ Men tend to be action-oriented, whereas women tend to be internally oriented; therefore, men often focus on competitive activities, while women often focus on inner feelings and relationships.

__ Men understand simple, direct language, whereas women understand the nuances of subtext and non-verbal cues.

__ Women can communicate with each other in ways that men miss.

PRACTICE THE VARIOUS KINDS OF ROMANCE

__ Be playful with and surprising towards your beloved.

__ Create opportunities that can become unexpected stories for your beloved to tell and retell.

__ Flirt skillfully and with understanding of its subtleties.

__ Give daily words of affirmation to your beloved.

__ Arrange to have quality time with your beloved.

__ Plan creative gift-giving for your beloved.

__ Serve your beloved unconditionally.

__ Touch your beloved daily, including hugs and kisses, holding hands, or massaging shoulders or feet.

AIM FOR GIVING TRUE UNCONDITIONAL LOVE EVERY DAY.

__ Practice friendship for its own sake.

__ Give gifts and service with no thought of receiving.

__ Look patiently for the joy that comes in giving with no thought of self.

MAKE A COMMITMENT, WHETHER OR NOT A MARRIAGE RITE IS PERFORMED.

__ Practice loyalty, no matter how others behave.

__ Before marrying, ask yourself the four marriage questions.

__ Base your marriage on love and friendship for their own sakes, rather than on the pleasure or usefulness of your beloved.

__ Let go of your criticisms, especially those that can turn into contempt.

__ Practice kindness and generosity in all that you think, say, and do.

RECOGNIZE THAT HAPPINESS COMES FROM A LIFETIME OF LIVING RIGHT.

___ Practice the classical virtues described by Aristotle: courage, generosity, justice, friendship, and citizenship, among others.

___ Take Charles Murray's advice and watch *Groundhog Day* every few years.

___ Become the type of person who embodies Hugh Hewitt's seven gifts: encouragement, energy, enthusiasm, empathy, good humor, graciousness, and gratitude.

___ Create a balance wheel to see the gaps in your life; then implement a plan to bring more balance to it.

___ Aim for the joy that comes with constantly giving unconditional love.

Recommended Reading

Barry, Dave. (1995.) *Dave Barry's Complete Guide to Guys.* New York: Random House. (A humorous take on, not men, but guys.)

Buscaglia, Leo. (1996.) *Love: What Life is All About.* New York: Ballantine Books.
(One of the great feel-good speakers and writers, and a role model of living love. You may want to first check out this fun and moving YouTube video of his university talk on "The Art of Being Fully Human.")

https://tinyurl.com/sarvid6

Chapman, Gary. (2010.) *The Five Love Languages: The Secret of Love that Lasts.* Chicago: Northfield Publishing. (A simple, modern view of love. Light reading.)
De Angelis, Barbara. (1990.) *Secrets About Men Every Woman Should Know.* New York: Dell Publishing. (Although some of her advice does not apply generally to all men and women, she often provides worthwhile suggestions.)

Hewitt, Hugh. (2014.) *The Happiest Life: Seven Gifts, Seven Givers, and the Secret of Genuine Success.* Nashville: Nelson Books.

Murray, Charles. (2014.) *The Curmudgeon's Guide to Getting Ahead: Dos and Don'ts of Right Behavior, Tough Thinking, Clear Writing, and Living a Good Life.* New York: Crown Publishing Group.

Prager, Dennis. (2008.) *Happiness is a Serious Problem.* New York: HarperCollins.

Twitchell, Paul. (1970, 1989.) *Stranger by the River.* Third ed. Minneapolis: ECKANKAR.

Appendix I

Literary Excerpts

ANNA KARENINA by Leo Tolstoy

Translated by Constance Garnett in 1901

from Volume II, Chapter 21 [edited without ellipses]

[In this chapter, note how Tolstoy emphasizes Vronsky's focus on physical love (Eros) for Anna. That love is reflected symbolically in Vronsky's experience with the mare.]

The temporary stable, a wooden shed, had been put up close to the race course, and there his mare was to have been taken the previous day. He had not yet seen her there.

He opened the door, and Vronsky went into the horse-box, dimly lighted by one little window. In the horse-box stood a dark bay mare, with a muzzle on, picking at the fresh straw with her hoofs. Looking round him in the twilight of the horse-box, Vronsky unconsciously took in once more in a comprehensive glance all the points of his favorite mare.

She looked altogether, except across the shoulders, as it were, pinched in at the sides and pressed out in depth. But she had in the highest degree the quality that makes all defects forgotten: that quality was blood, the blood that tells, as the English expression has it. The muscles stood up sharply under the network of sinews, covered with the delicate, mobile skin, soft as satin, and they were hard as bone. Her clean-cut head, with prominent, bright, spirited eyes, broadened out at the open nostrils, that showed the red blood in the cartilage within. About all her figure, and especially her head, there was a certain expression of energy, and, at the same time, of softness. She was one of those creatures which seem only not to speak because the mechanism of their mouth does not allow them to.

To Vronsky, at any rate, it seemed that she understood all he felt at that moment, looking at her.

Directly Vronsky went towards her, she drew in a deep breath, and, turning back her prominent eye till the white looked bloodshot, she started at the approaching figures from the opposite side, shaking her muzzle, and shifting lightly from one leg to the other.

"There, darling! There!" said Vronsky, going up to the mare and speaking soothingly to her.

But the nearer he came, the more excited she grew. Only when he stood by her head, she was suddenly quieter, while the muscles quivered under her soft, delicate coat. Vronsky patted her strong neck, straightened over her sharp withers a stray lock of her mane that had fallen on the other side, and moved his face near her dilated nostrils, transparent as a bat's wing.

She drew a loud breath and snorted out through her tense nostrils, started, pricked up her sharp ear, and put out her strong, black lip towards Vronsky, as though she would nip hold of his sleeve.

"Quiet, darling, quiet!" he said, patting her again over her hind-quarters; and with a glad sense that his mare was in the best possible condition, he went out of the horse-box.

The mare's excitement had infected Vronsky. He felt that his heart was throbbing, and that he, too, like the mare, longed to move, to bite; it was both dreadful and delicious.

"All right," answered Vronsky, smiling; and jumping into his carriage, he told the man to drive to Peterhof.

Before he had driven many paces away, the dark clouds that had been threatening rain all day broke, and there was a heavy downpour of rain.

"What a pity!" thought Vronsky, putting up the roof of the carriage. "It was muddy before, now it will be a perfect swamp." As he sat in solitude in the closed carriage, he took out his mother's letter and his brother's note, and read them through.

Yes, it was the same thing over and over again. Everyone, his mother, his brother, everyone thought fit to interfere in the affairs of his heart. This interference aroused in him a feeling of angry hatred—a feeling he had rarely known before.

"What business is it of theirs? Why does everybody feel called upon to concern himself about me? And why do they worry me so? Just because they see that this is something they can't understand.

"Whatever our destiny is or may be, we have made it ourselves, and we do not complain of it," he said, in the word we linking himself with Anna. "No, they must needs teach us how to live. They haven't an idea of what happiness is; they don't know that without our love, for us there is neither happiness nor unhappiness—no life at all," he thought.

He felt that the love that bound him to Anna was not a momentary impulse, which would pass, as worldly intrigues do pass, leaving no other traces in the life of either but pleasant or unpleasant memories.

He felt all the torture of his own and her position, all the difficulty there was for them, conspicuous as they were in the eye of all the world, in concealing their love, in lying and deceiving; and in lying, deceiving, feigning, and continually thinking of others, when the passion that united them was so intense that they were both oblivious of everything else but their love.

He vividly recalled all the constantly recurring instances of inevitable necessity for lying and deceit, which were so against his natural bent. He recalled particularly vividly the shame he had more than once detected in her at this necessity for lying and deceit.

And he experienced the strange feeling that had sometimes come upon him since his secret love for Anna. This was a feeling of loathing for something—whether for Alexey Alexandrovitch, or for himself, or for the whole world, he could not have said. But he always drove away this strange feeling. Now, too, he shook it off and continued the thread of his thoughts.

"Yes, she was unhappy before, but proud and at peace; and now she cannot be at peace and feel secure in her dignity, though she does not show it. Yes, we must put an end to it," he decided.

And for the first time the idea clearly presented itself that it was essential to put an end to this false position, and the sooner the better. "Throw up everything, she and I, and hide ourselves somewhere alone with our love," he said to himself.

Volume III, Chapter 11

[In this chapter, note how Tolstoy emphasizes Konstantin Levin's awareness of the love of Ivan and his wife as it manifests beyond physical love, as affection within a family (Storge), shared activity and friendship (Philia), and true

*unconditional love (Agape). These loves are reflected
symbolically in the peasants' working of the hay.]*

In the middle of July the elder of the village on Levin's
sister's estate, about fifteen miles from Pokrovskoe, came to
Levin to report on how things were going there and on the
hay.

From the vague answers to his question how much hay
had been cut on the principal meadow, from the hurry of
the village elder who had made the division, not asking
leave, from the whole tone of the peasant, Levin perceived
that there was something wrong in the division of the hay,
and made up his mind to drive over himself to look into the
matter.

The arguments and the division of the haycocks lasted
the whole afternoon. When the last of the hay had been
divided, Levin, entrusting the superintendence of the rest to
the counting-house clerk, sat down on a haycock marked
off by a stake of willow, and looked admiringly at the
meadow swarming with peasants.

In front of him, in the bend of the river beyond the
marsh, moved a bright-colored line of peasant women, and
the scattered hay was being rapidly formed into gray
winding rows over the pale green stubble. After the women
came the men with pitchforks, and from the gray rows
there were growing up broad, high, soft haycocks. To the
left, carts were rumbling over the meadow that had been
already cleared, and one after another the haycocks

vanished, flung up in huge forkfuls, and in their place there were rising heavy cartloads of fragrant hay hanging over the horses' hind-quarters.

"What weather for haying! What hay it'll be!" said an old man, Ivan Parmenov, squatting down beside Levin. "It's tea, not hay! It's like scattering grain to the ducks, the way they pick it up!" he added, pointing to the growing haycocks. "Since dinnertime they've carried a good half of it."

"The last load, eh?" he shouted to a young peasant, who drove by, standing in the front of an empty cart, shaking the cord reins.

"The last, dad!" the lad shouted back, pulling in the horse, and, smiling, he looked round at a bright, rosy-checked peasant girl who sat in the cart smiling too, and drove on.

"Who's that? Your son?" asked Levin.

"My baby," said the old man with a tender smile.

"What a fine fellow!"

"The lad's all right."

"Married already?"

"Yes, it's two years last St. Philip's day."

"Any children?"

"Children indeed! Why, for over a year he was innocent as a babe himself, and bashful too," answered the old man. "Well, the hay! It's as fragrant as tea!" he repeated, wishing to change the subject.

Levin looked more attentively at Ivan Parmenov and his wife. They were loading a haycock onto the cart not far from him. Ivan Parmenov was standing on the cart, taking, laying in place, and stamping down the huge bundles of hay, which his pretty young wife deftly handed up to him, at first in armfuls, and then on the pitchfork. The young wife worked easily, merrily, and dexterously. The close-packed hay did not once break away off her fork.

First she gathered it together, stuck the fork into it, then with a rapid, supple movement leaned the whole weight of her body on it, and at once with a bend of her back under the red belt she drew herself up, and arching her full bosom under the white smock, with a smart turn swung the fork in her arms, and flung the bundle of hay high onto the cart. Ivan, obviously doing his best to save her every minute of unnecessary labor, made haste, opening his arms to clutch the bundle and lay it in the cart.

As she raked together what was left of the hay, the young wife shook off the bits of hay that had fallen on her neck, and straightening the red kerchief that had dropped forward over her white brow, not browned like her face by the sun, she crept under the cart to tie up the load. Ivan directed her how to fasten the cord to the cross-piece, and at something she said he laughed aloud.

In the expressions of both faces was to be seen vigorous, young, freshly awakened love.

ROMEO AND JULIET by William Shakespeare

[Please note how Shakespeare uses this first scene to establish how Romeo's friends see no further than one side of Eros, sexual love. The scene is full of bawdy language and sexual innuendo. On stage, Mercutio is often portrayed as a kind of frat boy, thrusting his hips and making fun of Romeo's passion.]

ACT II. Scene I.

A lane by the wall of Capulet's orchard. Enter Romeo alone.

Romeo. Can I go forward when my heart is here?
Turn back, dull earth, and find thy center out.

[Climbs the wall and leaps down within it.]

Enter Benvolio with Mercutio.

Benvolio. Romeo! my cousin Romeo! Romeo!

Mercutio. He is wise,
And, on my life, hath stol'n him home to bed.

Benvolio. He ran this way, and leapt this orchard wall.
Call, good Mercutio.

Mercutio. Nay, I'll conjure too.
Romeo! humours! madman! passion! lover!

Appear thou in the likeness of a sigh;
Speak but one rhyme, and I am satisfied!
Cry but 'Ay me!' pronounce but 'love' and 'dove';
Speak to my gossip Venus one fair word,
One nickname for her purblind son and heir,
Young Adam Cupid, he that shot so trim
When King Cophetua lov'd the beggar maid!
He heareth not, he stirreth not, be moveth not;
The ape is dead, and I must conjure him.
I conjure thee by Rosaline's bright eyes.
By her high forehead and her scarlet lip,
By her fine foot, straight leg, and quivering thigh,
And the demesnes that there adjacent lie,
That in thy likeness thou appear to us!

Benvolio. An if he hear thee, thou wilt anger him.

Mercutio. This cannot anger him. 'Twould anger him
To raise a spirit in his mistress' circle
Of some strange nature, letting it there stand
Till she had laid it and conjured it down.
That were some spite; my invocation
Is fair and honest: in his mistress' name,
I conjure only but to raise up him.

Benvolio. Come, he hath hid himself among these trees
To be consorted with the humorous night.
Blind is his love and best befits the dark.

Mercutio. If love be blind, love cannot hit the mark.
Now will he sit under a medlar tree

And wish his mistress were that kind of fruit
As maids call medlars when they laugh alone.
O, Romeo, that she were, O that she were
An open et cetera, thou a pop'rin pear!
Romeo, good night. I'll to my truckle-bed;
This field-bed is too cold for me to sleep.
Come, shall we go?

Benvolio. Go then, for 'tis in vain
'To seek him here that means not to be found.

Exeunt.

*[In this second scene, Shakespeare provides Eros as well, but
the more romantic side that opens the door to other kinds of
love. Eros in the best sense is integrated with higher forms of
love. Romeo and Juliet's love leads to tragedy like Tolstoy's
portrayal in Anna Karenina, because they are born trapped
in the feud between their families.]*

Scene II

Capulet's orchard. Enter Romeo.

Romeo. He jests at scars that never felt a wound.

Enter Juliet above at a window.

But soft! What light through yonder window breaks?
It is the East, and Juliet is the sun!
Arise, fair sun, and kill the envious moon,
Who is already sick and pale with grief

That thou her maid art far more fair than she.
Be not her maid, since she is envious.
Her vestal livery is but sick and green,
And none but fools do wear it. Cast it off.
It is my lady; O, it is my love!
O that she knew she were!
She speaks, yet she says nothing. What of that?
Her eye discourses; I will answer it.
I am too bold; 'tis not to me she speaks.
Two of the fairest stars in all the heaven,
Having some business, do entreat her eyes
To twinkle in their spheres till they return.
What if her eyes were there, they in her head?
The brightness of her cheek would shame those stars
As daylight doth a lamp; her eyes in heaven
Would through the airy region stream so bright
That birds would sing and think it were not night.
See how she leans her cheek upon her hand!
O that I were a glove upon that hand,
That I might touch that cheek!

Juliet. Ay me!

Romeo. She speaks.
O, speak again, bright angel! for thou art
As glorious to this night, being o'er my head,
As is a winged messenger of heaven
Unto the white-upturned wondering eyes
Of mortals that fall back to gaze on him
When he bestrides the lazy-pacing clouds
And sails upon the bosom of the air.

Juliet. O Romeo, Romeo! wherefore art thou Romeo?
Deny thy father and refuse thy name!
Or, if thou wilt not, be but sworn my love,
And I'll no longer be a Capulet.

Romeo. [aside] Shall I hear more, or shall I speak at this?

Juliet. 'Tis but thy name that is my enemy.
Thou art thyself, though not a Montague.
What's Montague? it is nor hand, nor foot,
Nor arm, nor face, nor any other part
Belonging to a man. O, be some other name!
What's in a name? That which we call a rose
By any other name would smell as sweet.
So Romeo would, were he not Romeo called,
Retain that dear perfection which he owes
Without that title. Romeo, doff thy name;
And for that name, which is no part of thee,
Take all myself.

Romeo. I take thee at thy word.
Call me but love, and I'll be new baptized;
Henceforth I never will be Romeo.

[...]

Appendix II

On Happiness

Aristotle's Nichomachean Ethics

Translated by W. D. Ross in 1908

Book I, Chapter VIII [edited without ellipses]

We must now inquire concerning Happiness.

Now there is a common division of goods into three classes; one being called external, the other two those of the soul and body respectively, and those belonging to the soul we call most properly and specially good.

In our definition we assume that the actions and workings of the soul constitute Happiness, and these of course belong to the soul. And so our account is a good one, at least according to this opinion, which is of ancient date, and accepted by those who profess philosophy.

Now with those who assert it to be Virtue (Excellence), or some kind of Virtue, our account agrees: for working in the way of Excellence surely belongs to Excellence. And there is perhaps no unimportant difference between conceiving of the Chief Good as in possession or as in use, in other words, as a mere state or as a working.

For the state or habit may possibly exist in a subject without effecting any good, as, for instance, in him who is asleep, or in any other way inactive; but the working cannot so, for it will of necessity act, and act well.

Now in the case of the multitude of men the things which they individually esteem pleasant clash, because they are not such by nature, whereas to the lovers of nobleness those things are pleasant which are such by nature: but the actions in accordance with virtue are of this kind, so that they are pleasant both to the individuals and also in themselves.

So then their life has no need of pleasure as a kind of additional appendage, but involves pleasure in itself.

For, besides what I have just mentioned, a man is not a good man at all who feels no pleasure in noble actions, just as no one would call that man just who does not feel pleasure in acting justly, or liberal who does not in liberal actions, and similarly in the case of the other virtues which might be enumerated: and if this be so, then the actions in accordance with virtue must be in themselves pleasurable.

Then again they are certainly good and noble, and each of these in the highest degree; if we are to take as right the judgment of the good man, for he judges as we have said.

Thus Happiness is most excellent, most noble, and most pleasant, and these attributes are not separated. For all these co-exist in the best acts of working: and we say that Happiness is these, or one, that is, the best of them.

Why then should we not call happy the man who works in the way of perfect virtue, and is furnished with external goods sufficient for acting his part in the drama of life: and this during no ordinary period but such as constitutes a complete life as we have been describing it.

Book VIII, Chapter III

There are therefore three kinds of friendship, equal in number to the things that are lovable; for with respect to each there is a mutual and recognized love, and those who love each other wish well to each other in that respect in which they love one another.

Now those who love each other for their utility do not love each other for themselves but in virtue of some good which they get from each other.

So too with those who love for the sake of pleasure; it is not for their character that men love ready-witted people, but because they find them pleasant.

Therefore those who love for the sake of utility love for the sake of what is good for themselves, and those who love for the sake of pleasure do so for the sake of what is pleasant to themselves, and not in so far as the other is the person loved but in so far as he is useful or pleasant.

And thus these friendships are only incidental; for it is not as being the man he is that the loved person is loved, but as providing some good or pleasure.

Such friendships, then, are easily dissolved, if the parties do not remain like themselves; for if the one party is no longer pleasant or useful the other ceases to love him.

Now the useful is not permanent but is always changing. Thus when the motive of the friendship is done away, the friendship is dissolved, inasmuch as it existed only for the ends in question.

This kind of friendship seems to exist chiefly between old people (for at that age people pursue not the pleasant but the useful) and, of those who are in their prime or young, between those who pursue utility.

And such people do not live much with each other either; for sometimes they do not even find each other pleasant; therefore they do not need such companionship unless they are useful to each other; for they are pleasant to each other only in so far as they rouse in each other hopes of something good to come.

Among such friendships people also class the friendship of a host and guest.

On the other hand the friendship of young people seems to aim at pleasure; for they live under the guidance of emotion, and pursue above all what is pleasant to themselves and what is immediately before them; but with increasing age their pleasures become different.

This is why they quickly become friends and quickly cease to be so; their friendship changes with the object that is found pleasant, and such pleasure alters quickly.

Young people are amorous too; for the greater part of the friendship of love depends on emotion and aims at pleasure; this is why they fall in love and quickly fall out of love, changing often within a single day.

But these people do wish to spend their days and lives together; for it is thus that they attain the purpose of their friendship.

Perfect friendship is the friendship of men who are good, and alike in virtue; for these wish well alike to each other qua good, and they are good themselves.

Now those who wish well to their friends for their sake are most truly friends; for they do this by reason of own nature and not incidentally; therefore their friendship lasts as long as they are good—and goodness is an enduring thing.

And each is good without qualification and to his friend, for the good are both good without qualification and useful to each other.

So too they are pleasant; for the good are pleasant both without qualification and to each other, since to each his own activities and others like them are pleasurable, and the actions of the good are the same or like.

And such a friendship is as might be expected permanent, since there meet in it all the qualities that friends should have.

For all friendship is for the sake of good or of pleasure— good or pleasure either in the abstract or such as will be enjoyed by him who has the friendly feeling—and is based on a certain resemblance; and to a friendship of good men all the qualities we have named belong in virtue of the nature of the friends themselves; for in the case of this kind of friendship the other qualities also are alike in both friends, and that which is good without qualification is also without qualification pleasant, and these are the most lovable qualities.

Love and friendship therefore are found most and in their best form between such men.

But it is natural that such friendships should be infrequent; for such men are rare. Further, such friendship requires time and familiarity; as the proverb says, men cannot know each other till they have 'eaten salt together'; nor can they admit each other to friendship or be friends till each has been found lovable and been trusted by each.

Those who quickly show the marks of friendship to each other wish to be friends, but are not friends unless they both are lovable and know the fact; for a wish for friendship may arise quickly, but friendship does not.

About the Author

Mark Andre Alexander has a B.A. in English and an M.A. in Organization and Management Development. He works in Silicon Valley helping people take their next step. He's a happy soul, a composer and musician, and likes to make people laugh.

Occasionally he publishes articles and books. He's married to a woman who improves him just by being present, and he believes everyone is on a journey to learn how to give and receive **divine love.**

MarkAndreAlexander.Com

Subscribe to the *Creating Your Life* YouTube channel.

Books in the series *A Lifetime of Learning*
Creating Your Life: A Lifetime of Learning, Book 1
Money and Wealth: A Lifetime of Learning, Book 2
Sex and Romance: A Lifetime of Learning, Book 3
Mozart and Great Music: A Lifetime of Learning, Book 4

Forthcoming topics in the series include Shakespeare, great literature, the ancient Greeks, language, rhetoric, law, liberty, virtue, vice, education, training, science, truth, soul, and spirit.

Other books
Handbook for Advanced Souls: Eternal Reminders for the Present Moment

Public domain works edited by Mark Andre Alexander
Shakespeare's Law and Latin by Sir George Greenwood
The George Greenwood Collection
Hamlet and the Scottish Succession by Lilian Winstanley

THE SCHOOL OF
PYTHAGORAS™

If you want something to work,
you've got to put your love into it.
Harold Klemp

www.ingramcontent.com/pod-product-compliance
Lightning Source LLC
Chambersburg PA
CBHW071856020426
42331CB00010B/2544